W9-BNY-124

Saint Peter's University Library
Withdrawn

The Writing of
Peter Abrahams

Kolawole Ogungbesan

AFRICANA PUBLISHING COMPANY
A division of Holmes & Meier Publishers, Inc.
NEW YORK

First published in the United States of America 1979 by
AFRICANA PUBLISHING COMPANY
30 Irving Place, New York, N.Y. 10003.

Copyright © 1979 K. Ogungbesan
All rights reserved. No part of this publication may be
reproduced or transmitted in any form or by any means,
electronic or mechanical, including photocopy, recording,
or any information storage and retrieval system, without
permission in writing from the publisher.

Library of Congress Cataloging in Publication Data

Ogungbesan, Kolawole.
  The writings of peter abrahams
  Bibliography: p.
  Includes index
  1. Abrahams, Peter 1919 – Criticism and interpretation
  I. Title
PR369.3.A2Z8 1979   823   78-26133

ISBN 0–8419–0472–3
ISBN 0–8419–0480–4 pbk.

Printed in Great Britain

Contents

2
369.3
A 2
8
779

Acknowledgements

The publisher is grateful to J. Farquharson Ltd for permission to reproduce extracts from: *A Night of Their Own*, published by Faber and Faber; *A Wreath for Udomo*, published by Faber and Faber; *Dark Testament*, published by George Allen and Unwin Ltd; *Mine Boy*, published by Faber and Faber; *Return to Goli*, published by Faber and Faber; *Song of the City*, published by Dorothy Crisp and Co.; *Tell Freedom*, published by Faber and Faber; *The Path of Thunder*, published by Faber and Faber; *This Island Now*, published by Faber and Faber; *Wild Conquest*, published by Faber and Faber.

Introduction

Peter Abrahams was born on March 19, 1919 in Vrededorp, a Johannesburg slum. His father traced his line to the Ethiopian imperial dynasty. His mother, a Coloured, was the widow of a Cape Malay. The Coloureds (in South Africa the word is always written with a capital C) are the descendants of the blacks and the earliest white settlers. They live mainly in towns and cities all over South Africa, although their greatest concentration is in the Cape Province, where they number about half of the total population. After emancipation, the Cape Coloureds were accorded 'the privilege of the white blood in their veins' and had the same rights as the whites, including that of sending representatives to the provincial Parliament. But they lost this right in 1910 when the Act of Union amalgamated all the provinces into the Union of South Africa, and their status has steadily declined since then.

The Coloureds are regarded by the Whites as little better than the Blacks; they, in their turn look down on the Blacks, and until very recently refused to make a common political cause with them. They look up aspiringly to the Whites, and those among them who are very light-skinned usually 'pass' into the White group. Abrahams noticed in them the desperation and fear of a threatened species:

> Culturally, the Coloureds have no past, no tradition that goes to a time beyond the coming of the White man. They lack, as a group, the cohesive stability of the other groups. They are the most prejudiced and colour conscious of all the non-White groups.[1]

Abrahams made his debut as a poet and in fact, has to his credit a collection of poems entitled *A Black Man Speaks of Freedom* (1940) written before he left South Africa and published before his prose. Not unexpectedly, considering his age, the poems are unpolished although they never lack energy. One typical poem, titled *For Laughter*, is a pointer towards Abrahams' development as a writer, especially his ambition to surmount the daily frustrations of non-white living in South Africa:

I have learned to love
Burningly
With the fiercest fire;
And I have discarded humility
And the 'Will of God',
And the stories of my wise teachers.
Arming myself with the wretchedness
In every plain man's life,
And in all the tomorrows of my soldiers
I battle on behalf of that freedom
That will restore the laughter of man.[2]

Abrahams' aspirations drove him into exile in 1939, at the age of nineteen. But he himself has acknowledged the deep psychological wound he received before he ran away.

I had come away charged with bitterness against the whites of that land in particular and all whites in general. Life there had allowed me no self-respect, no dignity. And I had left suffering from a colossal inferiority complex, and carrying a huge chip on my shoulders.[3]

Before long, Abrahams succeeded in overcoming the bitterness, but it is doubtful if he ever outgrew the inferiority complex; it is difficult to explain otherwise his preoccupation with the theme of the black man's attempt to regain his manhood and self-respect as a precondition of achieving true independence. Abrahams believes that until this is done it will not be possible for the black man to mix with the white man on a personal level. His novels examine the different ways of reaching this goal.

Abrahams' vision is, as he puts it in *Mine Boy*, of 'man without colour', a world in which every man will be judged as an individual and where colour will be irrelevant. This explains the sentimental posture of his first novels—*Song of the City* (1943), *Mine Boy* (1946), *The Path of Thunder* (1948),

2

and *Wild Conquest* (1951)—where he sets the freedom of the mind over and above political independence. True freedom is of the spirit and is more difficult to achieve than political freedom. To achieve this spiritual freedom, the black heroes of his early novels forsake their restrictive tribal background for the white man's world of the city, the mines and the universities. Abrahams sees Westernisation as the only valid destiny open to the Africans, because he believes that it is on the white man's own ground that the black man should stand up to him if he is to be considered his equal and wishes to regain his self-confidence. This explains the emphasis placed on interracial love in the earlier novels: on the personal level it is the real test of race relationships; it is a symbol of the freedom of the mind from hatred and fear, a negation of the herd instinct as represented in the traditional societies by tribalism and, in the modern states, by apartheid.

> There are those who say that the world will not be free and happy—and I agree—until nations stop fighting other nations and nations stop oppressing other nations. The national intermarriage, whether between white and black or between pink and red, is a mirror of this highest form of world nationalism when man will really be free.[4]

Abrahams married a white woman soon after he settled down in Britain in 1941. But the past was not to be so easily laid to rest. He had to take his wife to France in the first days of their marriage in order to work out a lasting basis for their union. They lived among the peasants near Nemours, where their son was born. Abrahams claims to have been spiritually strengthened by the experience:

> It was there, among the French peasants, that I had come to realise the absurdity of colour judgements of any kind. I had found there the same prejudices and superstitions, the same 'backwardness', the almost tribal ways of living of Africa. This was the white counterpart of what made the whites of African call the dark folk there 'uncivilised'. In that village (Paley), race and colour had fallen into their proper places for me.[5]

Abrahams had been introduced to Marxism in his college days at St Peter's and soon became involved with the Communist Party in Britain. They were the only people prepared to offer him a job, in their book distributing agency. Very soon, however, and perhaps inevitably, he got into trouble with the communists, because he refused to submit his first two books for the party's clearance before publication. In return both *Dark Testament* and *Song of the City* received scathing reviews in *The Daily Worker* which resulted in Abrahams' breaking with the communists. In any case, he believed, the sort of control which they wanted to exercise was too much like what obtained in South Africa, and he felt that, like the colour bar from which he had fled, Marxism was inhibiting his desire to see the world and people in the round. Yet, his involvement with communism had a deep and lasting influence on his art:

> As a result of it I had realised that people, individual people, would always be more important than causes for me. My business as a writer was with people, with human thoughts, conflicts, longings and strivings, not with causes. Painfully, I was slowly groping to a view of life that transcended my own personal problems as a member of one oppressed group of humanity. I felt that if I could see the whole scheme of things with the long eye of history I might be able to fit the problems of my own group into the general human scheme and, in doing so, become a writer.[6]

Wild Conquest (1950) was the immediate product of this new personal and artistic creed. Abrahams believed that at last he had achieved a whole, rounded vision, and he pronounced satisfyingly after completing the novel: 'there was room for growth both as a man and a writer'.[7] On British radio he stated his new views about the colour problem, an eloquent statement which has remained the cornerstone of his art:

> Life is lived on more than one level. That is the first thing to be said. Everything that follows hinges on

4

that. Second, and equally important, is to state clearly that I am a coloured man, a Negro. If that were not necessary, the making of this statement would not be necessary. For if what follows had been said by a white man, it could, and in many places would, be dismissed in one form or another as yet a further manifestation of racial prejudice. As it is, I shall in all probability be accused of being a Negro who is anti-Negro. That is an accusation I must risk.

In a sense, this is my declaration of independence, my deliberate revolt against both black and white. For years I have found the burden of oppression by both wearisome and stifling. Now I would be rid of it. As a writer, my work demands this liberation if I am to see more clearly, to understand more wholly; as a human being it would add a completely new dimension of both pain and joy to the business of living. Here, then, is my declaration. If it is a spear, let it draw my own blood![8]

Abrahams' declaration of independence from both black and white was meant to enable him to criticise the two. In fact his focus changed in his subsequent works. Beginning with *Wild Conquest* Abrahams fixed his gaze firmly on the blacks and became more concerned with their fate. The premise of his argument was that oppression constitutes a greater psychological threat to the blacks than to their white oppressors. Everywhere on earth, he said, the black man carries a heavy burden of colour which threatens him both physically and spiritually. What Abrahams considered most terrifying is that the black man is fast adapting himself to the colour bar by opposing the white bigots' race hatred with hatred against all whites: 'So many have changed so much that they have lost the magic of the dream that carried them on that uphill journey till "they lifted themselves up by their own bootstrings". Large numbers of Negroes today counterpoise a black humanity against a white humanity.'[9] Abrahams thus pitched himself against *négritude*, the African personality, and other expressions of black pride because he believed that in order to regain his dignity, the black man must transcend the colour situation and live on the highest plane, as a man:

> On that level no Negro would be either proud or ashamed of being a Negro. And in his fight to be free he would not counter bigotry with more bigotry, prejudice with more prejudice. He would know that to do so would be to lose for his fight its contact with history, with the 2,000-year-old journey of man from darkness to the stars. And if he loses that contact, the battle will be lost, though won.[10]

The validity of these attitudes, formed in the freer atmosphere of England, could only be tested in South Africa, 'the battlefield of race hatred'. So Abrahams' visit, sponsored by the London *Observer* to report on conditions in the country of his birth, immediately assumed greater proportions. His six-week stay in South Africa was a traumatic experience. Conditions had worsened considerably since he left. *Return to Goli*, his account of the visit, is his most bitter book, but also the most vital clue to the development of his art. He was appalled by the conditions of the blacks: 'As I wandered about the country and saw how the Blacks lived in the Reserves, it seemed to me that one did not have to die to go to hell. This was hell. And the sun was shining from a clear sky.'[11] After an absence of close to fifteen years, his memory was becoming hazy. The second time around, it was like waking into a nightmare. He was palpably relieved to leave South Africa, even more so than in 1939.

Abrahams really grew up after this visit. One of the signs was that he proceeded immediately to write his autobiography. In order to be truly objective about the outside world one needs to undergo a period of intensive self-examination. The trip to South Africa forced Abrahams to take a journey into himself, into his origins, to determine his attitudes to life. His autobiography, *Tell Freedom* (1954) received universal acclamation, and remains the best among the profusion of autobiographies by South African non-whites. Abrahams' creative writing also entered a new phase. Henceforth he wrote only overtly political novels. His stay must have convinced him that the abject plight of the Africans, in a country where they form the majority, derives from their lack of political power. This awareness was probably strengthened when on his way back to Britain Abrahams stopped in Kenya, another plural society, where he met Jomo Kenyatta who in London had been, like most African intellectuals, a bitter opponent of colonial imperialism, quite as uncompromising as his friend Kwame Nkrumah, then Prime Minister of the Gold Coast. Kenyatta said to Abrahams: 'Tell me man, would it be such a crime if I, the leader of the majority of this country, were to be made Prime Minister? Would it be such a crime?'[12]

Although his vision remained essentially unchanged, Abrahams' approach altered radically. The main argument in the political novels—*A Wreath for Udomo* (1956), *A Night of Their Own* (1965), and *This Island Now* (1966)—is that political independence is a prerequisite of spiritual freedom. Abrahams' steadfast conviction that 'the most pressing need of the sensitive Black youngster' is 'to meet on terms of a social equality with Whites'[13] is examined within three different political situations—colonialism in *A Wreath for Udomo*, the colour bar in *A Night of Their Own*, and neo-colonialism in *This Island Now*. Instead of his earlier insistence on interracial love Abrahams now highlighted the virtues inherent in the idea represented by the Commonwealth, a committee of nations which respect one another's separate identities while combining, in spite of racial differences, in the pursuit of mutual progress and world peace.

Of all the plural societies Abrahams found Jamaica closest to this ideal, a conclusion with which most black Jamaicans would probably disagree. In 1955 he was sent to Jamaica by the Colonial Office to write a popular history of the island. His book, *Jamaica: An Island Mosaic* (1957), somewhat embarrassing in its purple passages, show how much he felt attuned to the island and its people. In his preface to the book he enthused: 'It was in the hills of Upper Trelawny, while living among the peasant hill-folk that I realised what an important symbol Jamaica was in our race-ridden world.'[14] Spelt out, this symbol was no less than Abrahams' original vision of 'man without colour':

7

> I had been born and brought up in a multi-racial society where the present was ugly and the future promised to be uglier. There the problems of race and colour, perhaps the key problems of our century, were so riddled with fear and hate that they seemed beyond any but the most terrible and bloody solution.
>
> In Jamaica, and in my exploring of its past and its problems, I had seen the solution of that problem. The Jamaicans had lived out the multi-racial problem and were now reaching a stage where race and colour did not matter, only a person's worth as a person. In this they are far ahead of most of the rest of the world; have much to teach the rest of the world.[15]

In 1959 Abrahams returned to Jamaica with his family, and has been living there since. He is a regular commentator on Jamaican radio, writes for *Holiday* magazine, and is editor of the *West Indian Economist*.

It is not difficult to see why Jamaica has become so important to Abrahams: gradually, people of diverse origins have come to accept one another as human beings. In an essay entitled *The Real Jamaica*, written against the background of Jamaica's independence on August 5, 1962, amidst wild rejoicings by all its people, Abrahams applauded Jamaica's progress, especially when compared with the fratricidal killings which marked independence in the Congo (Zaire). Abrahams found that even the Chinese, whom he had always thought unassimilable, have been integrated into the Jamaican melting-pot: 'In Jamaica, and in the stumbling and fumbling reaching forward of its people, is dramatised, almost at laboratory level, the most hopeful image I know of the newly emerging under-developed world.'[16]

Himself such an incurable optimist, all his books are open to the future, based on his belief that change is inevitable, a natural process. This is why the image of the day assumes such symbolic significance in his novels. The implication is that although the black people in South Africa are passing through a long night, their ordeal will not last for ever: after the night

8

inevitably comes the dawn. Abrahams thinks that it will be a glorious dawn if the whites and the blacks can co-operate peacefully to work towards that day.

NOTES

¹ Abrahams, *Return to Goli* (Faber and Faber, London, 1953), p. 57.
² Quoted in G. M. Miller and Howard Sergeant, *A Critical Survey of South African Poetry in English* (Balkema, Capetown, 1957), p. 146.
³ *Return to Goli*, p. 14.
⁴ Abrahams, *The Path of Thunder* (Faber and Faber, London, 1952), p. 93.
⁵ *Return to Goli*, p. 31.
⁶ *Ibid.*, p. 17.
⁷ *Ibid.*, p. 18.
⁸ *Ibid.*, pp. 18–19.
⁹ *Ibid.*, p. 21.
¹⁰ *Ibid.*, p. 27.
¹¹ *Ibid.*, p. 108.
¹² Abrahams, *Colonialism on Trial: The Kenyatta Case, Nation*, 177 (July 11, 1953), p. 32.
¹³ *Return to Goli*, p. 48.
¹⁴ Abrahams, *Jamaica: An Island Mosaic* (HMSO, London, 1957), p. xiv.
¹⁵ *Ibid.*, pp. 260–1.
¹⁶ Abrahams, *The Real Jamaica, Holiday*, 33 (March, 1963), p. 98.

Chapter One

Dark Testament

Dark Testament,[1] Abrahams' first volume of fiction, is a collection of sketches most of which were written before he left South Africa in 1939. The book is divided into two. The first eight sketches are reminiscences, beginning from the writer's schooldays and progressively portraying the growing awareness of the maturing youth; the remaining five pieces (each òf which is considerably longer than even the longest of the reminiscences) are called stories and are meant to be fictional. However, it is most unhelpful to insist on a hard and fast division between the two component parts of the book. *Dark Testament*, in spite of its apparent formlessness, possesses an underlying unity. The major theme is the growing of the artist, from the opening story, 'I remember ...', where Abrahams voices his commitment to art, to the concluding story, *The Virgin*, where, in despair, the artist decides to commit suicide. The other stories record his progressive disillusionment as he slowly discovers that the racial situation is too strong for him to maintain an uncorrupted commitment to art and that he cannot improve either his own condition or that of his society.

The book opens with the familiar classroom incident, in which each pupil stands up to tell his classmates about his ambition. Most of Abrahams' classmates want to be something easily realisable in South African terms—nurses, shopkeepers, even professors. Everyone knows of non-white doctors and nurses, even lawyers; and Professor Jabavu is famous all over the country. But young Abrahams wants to be 'something that was reserved for Europeans only':

> I have never heard of any non-European being what I wanted to be.
> 'I want to be a writer.'
> I waited for the effect. There was none. The teacher just sat smiling at me. A strange, half-

amused smile that made her look beautiful to me. She was good to look at even when she was not smiling. A light-coloured girl, who could pass for a white in a dim light.

'Why do you want to be a writer?'

My khaki shirt was torn in many places. It was very dirty. My body was not much cleaner. My khaki shorts had a great hole in the seat. Two girls behind me kept giggling at the visible parts of my bottom. My feet were cracked and bleeding. It was winter. There was a bump on my head from a recent fight.

'I want to be a writer so that I can write stories about everything. You know, like the stories in books. That will make me famous, and I'll have cakes and ginger beer for breakfast, and fish and chips for lunch, and a whole fowl at night. Then I'll be able to eat three times every day, and have shoes and a motor car, and live like the rich white people do. And then I want a collar and tie. That's why I want to write stories.'

For some time after she had told me to sit down the teacher laughed at me. Mostly with her eyes.

I remember that afternoon particularly well, because I fainted shortly afterwards. It was very difficult to revive me. When I came to I had to admit that I'd only had a slice of bread in two days. They gave me food, but that only made me ill, so I was sent to the General Hospital. I stayed there for a few weeks. They said I was suffering from starvation. Then they let me out to starve again...[2]

Abrahams has here set the scene for the whole drama of his life in South Africa, a drama in which the reality constantly interrupts the dream. The twin demons of loneliness and starvation will haunt the would-be artist, as indeed any non-white who has intellectual aspirations in South Africa. Deprivation is the basic denominator of non-white living. Comparing his lot with that of his childhood friends in another sketch, One of the Three, Abrahams writes: 'My life was pretty much the same. Poverty, want of woman's companionship, and the other things which the non-European South African of education knows so well.'³ Yet, in spite of the anguish of the educated African, Abrahams would not recommend the obvious alternative—a rejection of the white man's values, especially Western education.

There is a curious lack of cultural nationalism in Abrahams, perhaps because of his Coloured family background. He seems to have readily accepted that the state of the black man before the coming of the white man was an era of darkness, in which the black man was only slightly better than a beast. 'Do you know what it is to be a nigger in body?' he asks unabashedly in *Lonesome*, another sketch. 'Sub-human. And in mind a person? That is what I call loneliness.'⁴ The black intellectual's life-in-hell is not to be assuaged by his return to his cultural roots; rather Abrahams hopes he has permanently left that behind. His determination now is to win acceptance by the whites who are his cultural and intellectual peers. The familiar theme in black African writing of having been caught in the middle between traditional and Western values means little to Abrahams; instead, he laments his rejection by the whites and dwells on the threat that this rejection poses to his art. The ubiquitous phrase, *Reserved for Europeans Only* which dominates the pages of his writing as much as it dominates the thinking of South Africans is taken by Abrahams as a threat to both his person and his art.

Dark Testament resembles James Joyce's *Dubliners*. Joyce's main theme, the *fin-de-siècle* spiritual malaise in Ireland and the way it infected everything, above all private relationships, finds a counterpart in the racial policy of South Africa, the claustrophobic nature of which encloses the book as in life it threatens to fetter the spirits of the non-whites and successfully destroys any meaningful relationships between the races. Abrahams relies very much on atmosphere to convey his message, and very often the explicitness betrays a youthful writer. The situation in South Africa lends itself to cheap sentimentality, for it is deceptively easy to blame everything on the racial situation. Abrahams himself later came to realise this, and said so, and tried to do something about it. But in *Dark Testament*, the theme of racial discrimination is a hobby-horse. As the artist says in *Society*: 'The trouble with us coloured folks is that we are too quick to say a person is good for nothing.' The explanation, of course, is very simple—look at 'what's happening in South Africa, and how they treat us coloureds just like dogs'.[5]

Granted the inevitability of loss and deprivation as an over-riding theme in non-white South African writing (witness the deluge of autobiographies), Abrahams' approach in *Dark Testament* is remarkably subtle. Instead of merely recording incidents of deprivation, he emphasises them and gives them added poignancy, by making them a part of the process of growing up. The basic factor in all these stories is that life is a huge irony: the universal dichotomy between expectancy and achievement, dream and reality, is underscored for the non-white South African by the fact that his growing awareness increasingly alienates him from his environment. The simple but very pathetic tale of loss, *One of the Three*, about the break-up of the young artist's playgroup, illustrates well enough that South Africa is a Hardyesque world where the individual suffers in direct proportions to his awareness and his aspirations. The story also points the moral that apartheid poses a threat not only to individual aspirations but also to the collective will. Old age is normally the time for reminiscences and disillusionment, but the plight of the three friends shows how in South Africa the average non-white boy matures too quickly—a theme Abrahams later develops in *A Night of Their Own*.

The Old Watchman, another story of loss and dis-illusionment, is more successful because it is sifted through two consciousnesses, that of the old man and that of the artist. The old watchman, like the artist in *One of the Three*, looks back (over a time distance considerably longer than the artist's) to his youth, and remembers a time of happiness and innocence, when, as an apprentice clerk, he looked forward to a fairly secure future happily married to Sal. Suddenly, his world caved in: the girl, in deference to her filial duty, could not marry him. However, she did not part from her lover without bestowing a gift on him:

> She gave herself completely and utterly, and in that I saw God. For three days I lived the perfect life. I

13

knew what happiness was. My room was our heaven, and we were both terribly happy. I told her it was not humanly possible to be so happy. She only smiled, and said: 'Let us drink while we may, for soon we die.'[6]

The girl's short-term morality extends to all aspects of South African life, not least of all the artistic, where it encourages the short story instead of the longer work of art, the documentary and journalistic instead of the deeply creative. More than that, the lovers' exhausting three-day fiesta dictated its own sterility, the anxiety being to capture life while one could, because one knew that it would not last. On the creative level, it kills the artistic urge too, for the writer is only too anxious to live while he can, instead of sitting down to reflect on his experience, or giving it artistic shape.

The variety of approach in these sketches, in spite of the basic similarity in theme, shows Abrahams at so early a stage a would-be master of the short story. It is thus unfortunate that he did not sustain this longer, before jumping into the world of the novel where his main failures, as we shall see, are often those of a featherweight parading as a heavyweight. The most successful story in *Dark Testament* is *Love*, whose themes are, once again, love and its loss, and the defeat of hope. But here the theme operates on several levels. First we have the theme of innocence and experience, fundamental to *One of the Three*, in the story of Abrahams and his friend, Cockeye, who used to laugh at the old hunchback, Aunt Margaret. But as the two youths quickly learned the bitter lessons of life, they couldn't really laugh again. Their loss of innocence is dovetailed into that of Sis, Aunt Margaret's only child, a girl who sought to escape the arduous and unrewarding job for the local white 'baas' by going out with Joe, a fine flashy fellow with plenty of money in his pocket. The affair cost her her life, at childbirth. Thus Aunt Margaret had to work harder to take care of herself and her sickly grand-daughter.

Aunt Margaret's hump is a hump of love, and this supplies the clue to the title of the story. It is truly a love story, as we watch Ellen's growth balanced by the growth of her grandmother's hump. Then the screw is turned tighter in this life of blighted hope. Just as Ellen is old enough to look after herself and her grandmother, Aunt Margaret loses again—suddenly. Her best friend, Aunt Celia, tells the rest of the story to the artist—thus distancing it further than the double consciousnesses used in *The Old Man*—who has just returned from a journey into the world:

> '... Yes, chile, and then, when all her worries and troubles were near over, God says "Come to me, Ellen, come to your Father". You know what the doctor fellows say? They say TB. Just think of it. You've been to school and college, chile. You know 'bout all this. Margaret looked so well after her and they come and say TB. Disgraceful! Well, she died, and we buried her, and we was terribly sorry. But Margaret took it bad. She says "It's the will of the Father", and "Thy will be done. But it's so heavy, Lordy, so heavy!" After that she never spoke. She just sat down in her room. Sometimes she'd drink a bit of coffee if I brought it to her. Then one day she got up and said "Ellen", and fell down. That's all there is, chile.' The old woman turned away to wipe her eyes with her apron.
>
> The translation from the Afrikaans of Vrededorp robs the old woman's words of their strength...
>
> Before I left Vrededorp I went to the cemetery and stood over the little hump on the back of the earth. Under it Aunt Margaret was buried. I understood the full strength of her love and her religion as I stood there.[7]

It must be religion, for God is love. Aunt Margaret's manner of sorrowing is sublime: the loss is total, and is made more poignant by the studied silence of the bereaved—and the artist. Abrahams has avoided cheap sentimentality here because we do not have Aunt Margaret detailing her own loss. We know how colossal it must have been, and the artist knows too, and wisely keeps his peace, in obedience to that golden rule of art—tact. The heavy-handed irony of the author's translation robbing the old woman's words of their strength is perhaps unnecessary, and tends towards sentimentality, but

Abrahams rescues the situation in the last paragraph, by keeping quiet. Words, as the old woman tells the artist, must reel under such an experience. The author acknowledges this by his own silent tribute at Aunt Margaret's graveyard—that little hump of earth. Abrahams does not often succeed in avoiding the sentimental, and 'tears flow freely' on almost every page of *Dark Testament*—this remains a perennial Abrahams trademark—but perhaps this is unavoidable in a situation in which 'there is always death in the air'.[8]

Abrahams' characterisation in *Dark Testament* is a pointer to the development of his art. It is true, in short pieces such as these sketches we cannot expect any real development of character. The point really is that Abrahams' characters are stereotypes, distinguished only by their ordinariness. There is Old Isaac, 'a good Jew', whose devotion and kindness do not provide sufficient security from the racial prejudice of the land. Pressed by his wife, Emily, he agrees to leave South Africa, but asks where they would go. The author comments: 'The question invited silence. The droning of the flies turned it aside.'[9] But the old Jew is not the only one bogged down in the social miasma of South Africa. The Reverend Johnson of *The Homecoming* is equally tied to his study, 'his holy ground', where 'he spent his time thinking and reading, and communing with himself and with God, as befitted a man called to the service of God'.[10] But his otherworldliness is hardly better disguised than Old Isaac's yearning to return to the Old Country—obviously Russia—from where he had fled to South Africa in the first instance. Reverend Johnson's deliberately slow movement, and the measured cadences of his exhortation, mark him as much a stereotype as the Reverend Stephen Kumalo in Alan Paton's *Cry, the Beloved Country* (1948). Abrahams does not really know his own people better than the white liberal. Characters in *Dark Testament*—and in virtually all of Abrahams' later works—are so wooden because they are portrayed with too much regard for their social milieu—Old Isaac is a Jew in the traditional role, a shop-keeper—and they never rise above the ordinariness of their stations in life.

Practically all the characters in *Dark Testament* are outcasts like the artist himself, perhaps because his own sufferings and predicament as a social outcast enable him to establish rapport with other outcasts; he understands and can recreate their feelings because they are remarkably similar to his. This would explain the predominance of Jews in *Dark Testament*. The fellow-feeling between the black artist and individual Jews, as between a Jew and a Boer in *Hatred*, is meant to convince us that the colour barrier, is artificial and will soon pass away. The true barrier, as Abrahams sees it, is economic. This is explicitly stated in two stories, *Colour*, and *Thanksgiving*. Abrahams' commitment to Marxism at this time is undoubtedly very deep, but is also so explicit as to flaw these stories as works of art. In *Thanksgiving*, his earnestness leads him to shouting slogans. After helping Annie, a black girl who works in a garment-making factory, mend her love affair with Leslie, also black, Margaret Josephs, the white secretary of the workers' union who handles the black girls' emotional problems, counsels: 'If you meet others who are also fighting for freedom, and if you plan your work, and work together, then it won't be so hopeless. Will you try it with us? You've everything to gain, and nothing to lose.'[11] As if toasting a milieu in which racial animosity will be submerged in class warfare, Leslie and Margaret grip one another's hands as a token of newfound racial amity; Annie and Leslie are reconciled and, hopefully, live happily ever after; and the two working girls, black and white, are both thankful. 'Soon they were lost in the stream of workers hurrying home to rest.'[12]

Not all the stories are as naïvely doctrinaire as *Colour* or *Henny and Martha*, and there are signs even at this time that Abrahams' romance with Marxism is doomed to an early death. The desparation with which he tries to convince the reader—and himself—of the validity of the Marxist reading of the South African situation shows that there is a deep inner uneasiness about the applicability of the Marxist equation to the racial problems in South Africa. But more than that, Abrahams' warm humanity, which pervades all the stories, inevitably sets him on a collision course with the Marxists, whose narrowly dogmatic approach often appears curiously inhuman. This is brought out in *Lonesome*, the most racy sketch in *Dark Testament*, whose urgency conveys very well

17

the intensity of Abrahams' feeling. He has just arrived in Cape Town, trying to find a way out of the country, feeling lonely, bitter and frustrated from the workings of the colour bar, when he meets this nameless white female comrade, to whom he recounts his own plight and his people's sufferings:

> I told her these things. Sitting in a non–European cafe where we went so that it would be all right.
>
> I was a little bit in love with her; or rather, her company. She could understand, and give me sympathy, and then interest me in the Mass Meeting. But I guess she wanted to get away to go to a show. So we rushed through the tea, and again she told me the Movement was doomed if young, intellectual leaders like myself were becoming defeatist. What did the comrades in the other countries do?
>
> They at least had someone to talk to. Some woman to understand. Sex can be got in the street. But companionship is something like a religion. A God.[13]

This is unabashed protest, whose very anger and bitterness could not successfully conceal its impotence, both physical and spiritual. The girl's attempt to emasculate him as a person parallels and intensifies that of society which paralyses him as an artist.

In a situation where the artist completely commits himself to his society but discovers that he is powerless to influence its course, desparation inevitably becomes despair, and in South Africa the impotence of the black artist in the face of the monolithic state makes despair an inevitable ingredient of life. In the two key stories in *Dark Testament* Abrahams argues that perennial frustration will lead from despair to the artist's annihilation. *The Testament*, strategically placed at the end of the reminiscences, is about the trial of a non–white for murder, the absolute crime, symbolising the artist's rebellion against the norms of his society. Throughout the harangues of the lawyers, the accused remains apparently indifferent and aloof: 'He was looking at the patch of sun on the window beyond it. His eyes looked far away.'[14] His fixed gaze may symbolise a longing for exile, or a contemption of nature and God, as opposed to the lurid court scene which symbolises South Africa as a whole. Earlier, the artist had remarked, on seeing the sun shining on a patch of grass: 'Wonder how that grass can live here. Nothing seems to be able to live.'[15] Now, in defiance of death, he refuses the abject plea of his lawyer, who tries to curry favour from the all-white jury by claiming that his client is below them:

> '. . . on earth. Yes. Nothing is more pathetic than to fit nowhere. Nothing is more pathetic than to be an outcast. And, gentlemen of the jury, when you return your verdict, remember this: you are dealing with a person whose life has made him what he is. We have imposed on him and his kind a set of foreign laws. Does he understand those laws? How clear have we made them to him? I submit, gentlemen of the jury, that in a fit of blind passion that he could not understand he did what he did. Then the horror of what he had done dawned on him and he was frightened. He ran without knowing where.'
>
> The lawyer turned to the little box and looked at him. His eyes were still on the window and the sunshine. He didn't seem to see or hear what was happening. He was so far away.
>
> 'Joe!' the lawyer said.
>
> He did not turn his eyes from the window.
>
> 'Joe!' Slowly he turned his face and looked at the lawyer.
>
> 'You did it, heh?' He nodded his head mutely.
>
> 'You are sorry you did it, heh?' He was silent.
>
> 'You were frightened, heh?'
>
> His hands gripped the side of the little box.
>
> 'No I'm not frightened! I'm not frightened any more! *You can do what you like! I'm not frightened of any of you any more!*'
>
> The next day the papers were full of it.[16]

There is a sharp contrast between the lawyer's plea 'on earth' with the accused fixing his eyes on the sun. He accepts responsibility for his action, and defiantly refuses to show remorse. In a final outburst, he asserts his humanity and dignity, although he knows that his assertion will cost him his life; by refusing to plead extenuating circumstances he has lost the chance of obtaining leniency from the jury.

But Abrahams argues further that there is, indeed, no alternative to death. This is the interpretation of *The Virgin*, the story to which he has deliberately invited attention by strategically placing it at the end of *Dark Testament*. It is the summation of all the dilemmas that have bedevilled the artist; at the same time, it contains the resolution of these dilemmas. *The Virgin* appears more historical than fictional, showing that interest in history which is evident in all of Abrahams' writings. The date is firmly set: August 31, 1939 (Abrahams left South Africa soon after the World War began). Earlier the artist had claimed, in Conradian terms: 'I have kept faith with a dream. Whether I get published or not is another matter, and whether I am bad or good.'[17] Now, six of his stories have been rejected, and it is becoming imperative to get published, for he is lonely and starving; he can commune only with dead artists—John Keats, Vincent van Gogh, Arthur Sterling —those who had, in life, been unable to make good in social terms. 'There was no one else to speak to. No living soul who would understand. So I spoke to them. They understood, but could not reply.'[18] The despair contained in the last sentence is heightened by his inability to alter the social system; his frustration is deepened by the fact that, to others who are also socially committed, the artist brings a peculiar weapon whose effectiveness can be, and has frequently been, seriously questioned. The dilemma of W. B. Yeats, the artist's urge to prove himself in 'something that all others understand or share', is particularly poignant in South Africa:

> They think I am a failure. All of them. Even those who love me. They look at my withered-away body, and I can see them shaking their heads in their minds. It is so everywhere.
>
> Some say, do this. Try to do this, or that, and that. And when I tell them I can't, they smile. I know what they think. Lazy. Good-for-nothing. Oh yes, I can read it in their eyes and their smiles. I can see it in their hearts.

I try to tell them that I write. That my work is just as important as theirs. And in many cases more important. Then they smile wisely. Temperamental. One can see it in their eyes. It is there. It hurts my heart, this smug wisdom even among the progressives.

But I am a failure. Ever since I can remember I have been writing. I have taken paper and pen and ink. On it I have poured out the deep cries that the people were too afraid to utter. Into it I have poured every last ounce of strength I had in my body. I tortured my mind so that there should be no mistake. No false note. No touch of dishonesty.

It is a big job, this. Bigger than breaking rocks with a hammer. Or building a road for rich people to travel along in shiny cars. But I am a failure. And this is the story of my failure. My world, my country, has no place for me.[19]

The only person who can understand, and seems to need him, is another type of artist—the prostitute, a girl named Rosie. After a three-day fainting spell, resulting from starvation and exhaustion, the artist revives and discovers the girl, who has stayed by his bedside throughout his illness, reading a collection of his stories, the tales told to him by the old watchman, to pass the time. 'I looked into her eyes, and there were tears in them. And hunger. And all my loneliness, and more.'[20] With this acknowledgement of empathy between the two, the artist's superiority complex is gone: 'I felt something that I had never felt before. I felt like an ordinary person.'[21] Rosie had even paid the doctor's bills, prostituting herself on his behalf, just as he had done on behalf of society. 'I had suffered much, but I had learnt nothing from it. It needed the suffering of a greater and stronger person to teach me something.'[22] What he has learnt is that too much social commitment can stifle art. Henceforth, he is going to learn to deal with universal problems: 'Let me write about these people. . . . Not as people who work and eat and sleep and drink and get drunk and fight because they lack education. . . . But as people with souls that are crying for understanding.'[23] This is the clue

21

SAINT PETER'S COLLEGE LIBRARY JERSEY CITY, NEW JERSEY 07306

to the meaning of the title of the story. On the obvious level, Rosie the prostitute is the virgin: although 'many men have held her in their arms' and 'pressed their lips to hers', she is a virgin because 'this was the first kiss. The first time she was kissed and kissed back as a human being.'[24] On a deeper level, it refers to the artist; for the first time he has discovered his true vocation. He is going to dedicate himself to art, write about all the people, refusing to be circumscribed by racial boundaries. He will endeavour to live up to that high conception of creativity which he envisioned at the beginning:

> What I mean is this. The doctor who delivers the woman of her child is doing a job. If he's a new one, there is some excitement in it. But it's still just a job ... But with you and me it's so different. It's the earth. Generations of earth. Centuries of earth. Timeless earth. It's the earth bursting loose slowly. Coming up and breaking up. Opening up. You know, like a ball of damp earth falling apart. And you see inside it. You see nothing. But it's beautiful to see it, although it's nothing ... That is what philosophers miss. That's why I hate them some-times.[25]

But Rosie's race is run in three days. Her heart gives way: 'It's the strain of the unnatural life I live,'[26] she had explained to the artist. However, she dies happily, knowing that she is no longer alone. For the artist also, the past has proved too strong; he, too, has reached the end of the road:

> I cannot stand any more. I have fought as hard as I could, but I cannot. Rosie went too soon. Yes. I'm a failure. Not because they keep sending me rejection slips. But because I haven't the courage to go on living now. But am I alone a failure? What about you. You helped to do this to Rosie and me. I hate you! I wish I could make you hate yourself as much as I do. Then perhaps those who will come after me would have a chance to live. Sure, I dramatised the most sacred thing in my life. For your benefit! Christ! Can you see yourself? Or are you so dead ...

so far gone ... What about you? You are the murderer! Your souls died long ago. I wandered through your world of civilisation and enlightenment. And found God in one of your outcasts...

Yes! Tomorrow you can print it!

FAILURE KILLS HIMSELF AND BLAMES SOCIETY![27]

Abrahams read the danger signals early enough, and fled from South Africa rather than commit artistic suicide by waiting for the social situation to stifle him to death. As he later explains in his autobiographical *Return to Goli*, because he had protested against the situation, he had not been able to earn a living, but his spiritual needs were more pressing. 'Life in that country had made me humourless, intense and bitter.'[28] The final impression of *Dark Testament* is that it is a humourless, intense and bitter book.

NOTES

[1] *Dark Testament* (George Allen and Unwin, London, 1942). All page references are to this edition.

[2] *Ibid.*, pp. 9–10.
[3] *Ibid.*, p. 14.
[4] *Ibid.*, p. 60.
[5] *Ibid.*, p. 47.
[6] *Ibid.*, p. 55.
[7] *Ibid.*, p. 26.
[8] *Ibid.*, p. 70.
[9] *Ibid.*, p. 87.
[10] *Ibid.*, p. 100.
[11] *Ibid.*, p. 117.
[12] *Ibid.*, p. 117.
[13] *Ibid.*, pp. 59–60.
[14] *Ibid.*, p. 75.
[15] *Ibid.*, p. 42.
[16] *Ibid.*, p. 76.
[17] *Ibid.*, p. 10.
[18] *Ibid.*, p. 144.
[19] *Ibid.*, p. 141.
[20] *Ibid.*, p. 156.
[21] *Ibid.*, p. 155.
[22] *Ibid.*, p. 156.
[23] *Ibid.*, p. 158.
[24] *Ibid.*, p. 159.
[25] *Ibid.*, p. 56.
[26] *Ibid.*, p. 157.
[27] *Ibid.*, p. 159–60.
[28] *Return to Goli*, p. 14.

Chapter Two
Song of the City

Song of the City[1] holds no surprises for anyone who has read *Dark Testament*. In his introductory biographical note to the earlier book Abrahams said: 'I have completed a novel. Done half a second, and a third of a third.'[2] This means that by the time he published *Dark Testament* Abrahams had finished *Song of the City*, written half of *Mine Boy* and a third of *The Path of Thunder*. Thus, while we may rightly expect maturity and competence in these books we know there will be no revolutionary departures, technically and thematically, from the first book. One story from *Dark Testament* is of special interest. Significantly entitled *From an Unfinished Novel*, it has strong links with *Song of the City* which reach through Abrahams' writing career. The setting of the unfinished novel is the highveld, which is also the setting of *The Path of Thunder* and *Wild Conquest*, and a part of the action of *Song of the City*. Abrahams has an eye for the countryside, as even the stories in *Dark Testament* testify, and although most of his descriptions do not go beyond the commonplace, he keeps his characters constantly in the company of nature. Furthermore, *From an Unfinished Novel* demonstrates that abiding interest in history which links all of Abrahams' writings.

The structural weakness of Abrahams' novels is foreshadowed in this short story. The wide sweep of its opening is more suitable for an epic—and Abrahams later adopts it with some measure of success in *Wild Conquest*—rather than the melodramatic story of a Coloured girl and a white man, which appears tagged to the setting. As a story, it doesn't even hold the dramatic possibilities of a liaison between a white girl and a Coloured boy, as Abrahams himself seems to acknowledge in *The Path of Thunder*. In *Song of the City*, Uys' fathering a baby by a coloured girl hardly raises any ripples. So, *From an Unfinished Novel* demonstrates that Abrahams is likely to bite off more than he can chew, that the vehicle is likely to be too heavy for the thin story it is meant to carry (in all his novels Abrahams is weak on plot).

In *Song of the City* materials for at least two novels are crammed into less than two hundred pages. The novel begins simply enough as a tale about the conflict between the traditional and the Western—which the opening of *From an Unfinished Novel* is all about—what Abrahams is later to attempt with better results, in *Mine Boy*, and, in a sense, the prototype of most African novels of the sixties. Maybe all would have been well if Abrahams had stuck to his plan. *Song* would not thereby have been a first-class novel, but it would have been confined to proportions more manageable for a young writer. Nduli, the central character, leaves home with sunrise—Abrahams' characters always have a great sense of timing—and arrives, like Xuma in the following novel, in the city at nightfall. The unstated question is how much of this 'home' would sustain him as he assumes his new life. The tale Abrahams is about to tell is, in the words of the old historian who sends Nduli on his way, 'the record of that journey' of the black man from the tribal past to the Western present.

Yet Abrahams does not exploit the full possibilities which this simple plot opens to him. For example, after his interview with the policeman who gave him a pass and a second name (up to this time the advice of the elders seemed to have worked), Dick Nduli could have been portrayed as a man with a split personality. The Western name takes precedence over the traditional, and gradually Nduli himself settles for the Western, as if demonstrating the increasing hold that Westernisation is exercising over his personality. Abrahams is either unwilling or unable to pursue a sustained psychological analysis of his central character; rather, he seems more interested in Nduli's physical progress, the journey itself, and all the effort is concentrated on bringing out—directly, and without the least subtlety—that this is a watershed in Nduli's life.

Nduli is a caricature and lacks any individuality. He gets a job, predictably as a domestic servant in the house of Professor Solomon Ashe, who happens to be white, liberal, a pacifist and a Jew. Not that employer and employee are ever allowed to rub against each other, except that Dick cannot understand the kindness of his employers (the white man's kindness always baffles the black man in the world of Abrahams), nor the liberalism which makes the Ashe family treat Doctor Timbata, a black man, as their equal. We are never allowed to draw our own conclusions about what is happening to Dick. He himself is always anxious to tell us how bewildering everything is and he bares his soul to the rest of the world in a letter written to his mother but read all over again to himself, for our benefit:

'Dear Mother, I have now been in the big city for nearly a month. I do not know if I like it or not. Last night a policeman stopped me. Mtini, he is thin as a reed, he lives in the same compound with me and Mbale, he says they always do it. Last week I went with Mbale to see a bioscope. You go into a big room with lots of chairs, you pay seven pennies to go in and you sit down and a big man with a whip whom they call Cheriff, goes up and down and makes people keep quiet. Then the lights go out and you see white people on the wall and you hear them speak. They also fight and shoot with guns. It's a very nice thing to see. In the evening yesterday a black man who was like a white man came in here and slept in the home of my master. Mtini looks like a man who is going to die. He spits blood. I am well. The white people here where I work are good. They give me plenty of food, and the white people of the cities do not beat you like the white one of the farms.' There it ended. He felt dissatisfied. There was so much more he wanted to say, but how can you say it on paper. He thought of something else to say. There was so much to say. He took a pencil stub out of his pocket and licked it. He thought for a while, then wrote slowly: 'I am lonely. There is no one to talk to. No one like a real friend, I mean, but there is a girl who has come to work next door, maybe we shall be friends. I would like it to be so. Your son Dick Nduli.'

He looked over the letter again and folded it. He thought of home and smiled dreamily. It would be good to be on the farms now, with no noises and no police and only the open country and cattle. And no streets to go across with motor cars trying to run over you, and there would be girls and you can drink beer without fearing the police. A heavy loneliness settled over him. He ached for something that he could not name. Something warm and soft. Something that would take the cry out of his heart so that it should not beat so loudly and sadly.[3]

The lack of technical innovation, as much as the predictability of much of the material, serves to remind us how thoroughly steeped Abrahams is in the Western literary tradition. However, the letter succeeds as an attempt to capture the jumbled thoughts and feelings of a newcomer to the city; the fear of the police, which runs through it, is a more successful attempt to create an atmosphere, because it is more subtle. Dick's nostalgia expresses itself in longing for a woman—the letter is addressed to his mother—and immediately (it is a recurring motif in Abrahams, this pert coincidence) everything falls into place, for Dick only needs to lift his head up from his letter to see the buxom girl who has been steadily watching him for a long time: 'It threw him into confusion. He did not know what to do. There was something imperious in her attitude. It commanded louder than words.'[4] There is always this imperiousness about Abrahams' women, but his men do not often have to worry about this, for the women are always forward (sometimes indelicately so), and always know what to do. Daisy does, because she is the daughter of the city; she is not only in the city, she is of the city, and her virtues—or lack of them—are city-bred.

Daisy is as vitally alive as most whores, and as bereft of individuality. Abrahams is no more successful in making us see her than in his attempt to render to us the meaning of the song of the city although Daisy tries so often to explain, and perhaps tries too hard. The meaning of the song is as simple as its origin, which Abrahams has supplied elsewhere. As a boy of fifteen, he had worked as a servant in a hotel; his working day began at five in the morning and ended after midnight:

In all the time I worked at the hotel, I never once walked through the streets of my city in daylight. And because of the silence of the streets during my passage to and from my work, I heard the drone of the city clearly: the deep hum without end that seemed to come from the very bowels of the earth. I called it the song of the city and spun a web of tired dreams to it. It became the companion of my dark journeys.[5]

Abrahams has here explained not only the beginning of the song of the city but also its meaning. And he does so with a simplicity that belies Daisy's persistent claim that the song is indefinable, even as she is trying to define it. The emphasis is on the song's impersonality. In the novel all references to it, and attempts to unravel its meaning, are made in the night. Very early in the novel we catch the artist himself, not any of the characters, giving expression to the song of the city and the meaning it had for him in his youth. The following are the opening paragraphs of Chapter Three *River of Race*:

On earth the personality of Johannesburg was expressed in a hum. Incessant. Monotonous. Wrenched from the bowels of the earth; creeping through the walls and windows, invading stillness and drowning it in the oppressing monotony.

That is the soul of night over Johannesburg. Over its suburbs. Over Vrededorp, slum home of the dark-skinned thousands, over Parktown, home of the wealthy Europeans; over Berea, predominantly Jewish; over Fordsburg, melting-pot of the poor whites.

The ceaseless hum of the night formed the common unit for Johannesburg. It invaded everywhere.

For it alone there is no colour, no wealth, no race, no creed. Almost it seemed to say: 'without me there can be no rich. No poor. No black. No white. No gold ... No city.'[6]

The emphasis is on the impersonality of the 'hum' of Johannesburg. The preoccupations of South Africa—colour, wealth, race, and creed—are lost in the hum. 'From the bowels of the earth came the song of the city, and on it, the lesser song of the Maraba,'[7] the native dance hall. The ceaseless hum which comes from the bowel of the earth drowns all human concerns; but more than that, it is the embodiment of life in the city, both happiness and sorrow, by both white and black. This is ultimately why no individual, no matter what his race, knows all of the song, and why the attempts in this novel to *live* the song are more successful than the attempts to explain it.

Abrahams' major problem in *Song of the City* is to fuse his two major themes: South Africa's response to the Second World War, and Dick Nduli's education; to marry the world of the drawing-room and the Maraba. And it is a problem which he fails to solve satisfactorily. In spite of alternating the chapters, and even making some characters operate (half heartedly) in the two worlds, he does not succeed in overcoming the weight of two unrelated dramas unfolding simultaneously—that is if Nduli's growth has any dramatic overtones at all. It is a measure of Abrahams' failure that Nduli's development, probably meant to be the weightier theme, takes second place to the story of the war. In fact, Abrahams' tense writing is more suitable to the momentum of a country caught at the crossroads of destiny than the development of a black native from rural setting to Western urbanisation.

The passages about South Africa's response to the war are the best in the novel, partly because Abrahams' journalistic style finds an appropriate subject here: short phrases, or jerky sentences at best, to report the incoherent or semi-coherent exhortations at huge meetings urging a call to arms, even in defence of neutrality. Here short sentences can be conveniently used, even over long passages, for the atmosphere is naturally tense and the style merely keeps in step with the mood. Chapter Seven entitled *Man of Sincerity*, opens:

> The undercurrent of the split in the Government was everywhere. The country was in a state of unrest. There were periodic eruptions. Then lulls. Then more eruptions. Then lulls. Fiery politics seared the country. There was trouble in the

police force. Secret organisations of a military and semi-military character reared their heads. Feeling ran high over the two Anthems. Unrest everywhere.

In Durban non-Europeans held huge meetings. In Cape Town non-Europeans held huge meetings. In Johannesburg non-Europeans held huge meetings. They called for the abolition of the colour bar. They called for the abolition of the pass-law. They called for freedom of movement. For better pay. For treatment as human beings.

In all the big cities Afrikaner Nationalists held huge meetings. They dressed in the garb of the old voortrekkers of history. They denounced war. They called for peace. For freedom from humiliation and insult. For honour for their national language and 'kultur'. Some promised a new Blood River. A new type of state and people.

In all the big cities Dominionites held huge meetings. They called to the fight for freedom. The fight for a way of life that must not die. For the culture and freedom that had been won through long and hard years of strife and labour. They echoed a great statesman and said the lights were going out everywhere, they must not all go out. South Africa must see that they do not all go out.

And in this storm a people swayed. And the warm sun streamed over the country. And the harvest was good. And the grass was green. And the good earth responded to the spade. And there were no pests or epidemics. Only a small cloud of locusts had been observed to fly from the East to the West without doing any harm.[8]

A great part of the success of the style here derives from the monotony, comparable to the monotony of the objects themselves—'huge meetings' everywhere, by different people who 'called for' essentially the same thing, a defence of their own interests. The phrase 'huge meetings' robs each gathering of all individuality, just as there is no individuality in the cloud of locusts which passes over the land. The threat from the locusts, although unrealised, underscores the destructive potentialities of the war looming in the horizon, also against the background of an indifferent universe.

Abrahams' intention is to show that the selfish considerations of the South Africans miss the issues at stake: the survival of Western civilisation and especially of personal freedom, its corner-stone. Obviously he considers these issues far too important to approve of the pacificism of Professor Ashe. Abrahams has no sympathy for Ashe at all, which is why the old professor of philosophy is made to look so stupid. The war fever is carried right into Ashe's drawing-room by his friend Richardson who, as an English-speaking South African, wants his friend to throw his weight (slight as it is physically and, perhaps, intellectually) behind efforts to get South Africa into the war on the side of the Allies. But the professor is hardly ruffled. Chapter Two, in which the two debate the merits of neutrality, is entitled *The Undertones . . .*, and displays one of Abrahams' more successful uses of irony. Abrahams knows his two 'civilised' characters and the world of the drawing-room where the dialogue takes place—it could well be in London. The subject, deeply controversial, is none the less discussed in undertones; Ashe's voice remains even more modulated throughout, as befits a man who looks at passionate problems dispassionately. The dangers of Ashe's pacificism in an embattled land are seen within his own house. Rachel, his elder daughter, is terribly lonely, has taken up knitting as an outlet for her frustrations, 'and all her thoughts and dreams and hopes were burnt out in flying needles and polite coldness'.[9]

Ashe's younger daughter, Naomi, deserves more attention, because she is the only one still vitally alive within Ashe's household. Also, she is aware of the dangers to which her home, under the guise of shelter and respectability, exposes her. Most important, she is the first in a long line of Abrahams' portraits of the artist-as-hero. Naomi is a pianist, and in spite of (if not together with) her youthfulness, this identification with art gives her a perception which other characters lack. Indeed, it is perhaps not perception at all, but an innocence which makes her emphasise all the time the superiority of the humane over the dogmatic. Yet Naomi is not a credible character, because she is not content to be just herself. Neither her innocence nor her role as the music-maker could have given her the penetration she shows in dealing with people, pointing out the weaknesses in their views of life. What Naomi does not know must have escaped Abrahams himself.

The problem must have been that Abrahams was at a loss as to how to embody his own standpoint in the novel without too heavy an authorial comment. So, he chose the most obvious way out—he devised a character, young (and, therefore, innocent) who is also an artist, and therefore perceptive—and used her as the vehicle to convey his own opinions. Naomi's ability to see through everyone is one of the novel's most implausible aspects. Her rejoinder to her father remains Abrahams' answer to the question of South Africa's stand during the war: no person or country could afford to be neutral when the stakes are so high. 'Like being a spectator while things are destroyed around you. It helps nobody. It's not human.' This is the criterion used to judge—and condemn—Hendrik Van der Merwe, the Minister for Native Affairs, the 'man of sincerity', who goes to consult his constituency about how he should vote in Parliament. Sincerity is not enough, and Abrahams condemns Van der Merwe's lack of courage. The Minister has to choose between his wife and his political career, and in spite of his anguish he chooses to safeguard his political future, bends to the anti-Semitic, anti-English, hate-mongering temper of his constituency, and votes for South Africa's neutrality. Ironically, his choice of neutrality does not save the country; rather, it brings the war into his own household. The woman who for three years of marriage has filled his life with 'love and fun and laughter' leaves him, condemning him for the rest of his life to isolation.

Myra Van der Merwe is the only character in the book who is given any individuality. Her hallmark is a generosity of heart which enables her to see the other sides of an argument while remaining firm about her own convictions, and a humaneness which knows no boundary of race and geography. She empathises with her Coloured housemaid, and voices the only concern for the baby begotten by the mentally retarded Uys and a Coloured girl who turns out to be Dick's sister. Her husband's feeling for his country is expressed in his love for the land itself, symbolised by the hill of granite to which he tries to relate whenever he looks out of his window and which he has always tried to reach since his youth. But Myra's love transcends the land itself and reaches to all people and their suffering. Placing human beings over and above what her husband calls 'duty', she leaves him to return 'home', as she persistently refers to England, but it is certain that, to her, home means more than a habitation.

> ... She saw her home and the things that made it home. The people. Their voices. Their smiles and their tears. Eyes and hands. Lips moving. And the words. And the earth and the sky. And behind them all she saw Van. Face coming and going. And the things they had done together. The little world they had built for themselves. A sweet little world it was. So quiet and peaceful. So touched with love and laughter. And the silences that are so precious. Not Africa. Not England. Not English people or Afrikaner people. Just a world. And just people...[11]

The other characters are just *not* living people; stereotypes, they can be described in a sentence or two. Ernst Cellier, the newspaper reporter, is a cynic masquerading as a deep thinker, but in reality is as shallow as anyone else. The clue to his personality is the pair of dark glasses he wears permanently in public, a mask of irony and cynicism. Dr Timothy Timbata is the educated 'responsible' black leader and intellectual who counsels a 'reasonable' approach to the race question, and plays into the hands of the authorities by advocating something remarkably similar to what has become known as a Bantustan homeland.

Abrahams is more sympathetic to Timbata's political opponent, the young Ndaba, whom we never see but whose views are touted by the Communist Roger Jones. Abrahams demonstrates the strength of his own convictions by making Roger Jones tear Timbata to shreds intellectually, ending in a triumphant condemnation of the latter's beliefs and life style: 'Ndaba has learnt something that no amount of book-learning can put into your heart, and that is that people who are subjected and desire freedom must desire it strongly enough

33

to stand up and fight for it. Nobody else will give it to them, no matter how eloquently they beg.'[12] Roger's Marxist beliefs also enable him to see through Ernst Cellier whom he treats with becoming condescension matching the latter's contempt for the world. Don't flatter yourself,' he contemptuously dismisses the cynic. 'The Marxist interpretation would declare you a corpse that should have been in the earth ten years ago. You're not even a good bourgeois. You're not a social animal; you are a perverted misfit.'[13]

Yet Roger Jones is not without his own failings, and it is a tribute to Abrahams' sincerity that when he puts him to the test in the discussion with Naomi he shows us the short-comings of communism—which is perhaps why *Song of the City* received such a scathing review in *The Daily Worker*. Naomi rebukes the dogmatic Roger:

> 'You know,' she said slowly, 'it's harder to under-
> stand you than it is to understand either Lee or Ernst.
> I think it's because everything you say comes from
> your head and not from your heart. There's always
> something to it. Something planned that leads in a
> very definite direction. I thought you were angry
> when you spoke to Ernst, when you quote that
> verse, but you were leading in a definite political
> direction again. Don't you sometimes long for the
> language of the heart? Not to be going any where
> but just to be drifting?' Again she watched the tired
> eyes and wished to know what feeling was behind
> them. She said: 'There must be a point of human
> contact with you somewhere.'[14]

Abrahams' failure to imbue his characters with humanity is most marked in Dick Nduli, the central character in the novel. Although he is the first character to be introduced, he remains nameless for some time, a device Abrahams uses later, with some success, in *A Night of Their Own*, a cloak-and-dagger story. Nduli is fleetingly commented upon by people across the racial line, yet what we have is nowhere near a complete picture, mainly because Abrahams is more interested in what Nduli represents than in his individuality. Through him we are meant to see what happens to the native rustic fresh to the city. Abrahams' political preoccupation soon detracts our attention from Nduli, and he is lost in weightier matters. Nduli should interest us, as the first of Abrahams' passive heroes. Otherwise, the transformation in his personality is not adequately motivated. The first crisis of his life is also the most traumatic: he is arrested—wrongly, of course—and convicted, fortunately with an option of a fine which Daisy promptly pays. Suddenly, the excited man from the farm is gone; now Dick wants to know things, especially how not to fear the white man.

> Dick thought about the young man who had no fear and who had said the white man wanted them to have fear. Why? Why? What did the old men say about it? He thought hard. The old men had been right in everthing and if they had said anything about this it would be right too. But they had told him nothing about this fear the white man wanted him to have. Did they know about it? They must know about it. How could a young one, one who is as young as himself, know about it, and the old men not. They must know. Maybe they forgot to tell him. Maybe they did not want him to know. But he will write and ask them and they will tell him. That one is so young. How could he know and the old men not. The old men must know and he will get them to tell him.[15]

Abrahams' point is not, contrary to what one easily suspects, that familiarity with the white man will breed in the black contempt for his rulers, but that a knowledge of the white ways will open the gate to the dignified present for the black. The old men, who represent the tribal past, can no longer claim to be the repository of wisdom; what they know is no longer relevant to the present. In fact, a mere youth in the city is wiser in the ways of the world than the wisest tribal man. The author's message is not clear to his character. Worse, Nduli's life in the city hardly bears out the message. The death of his friend Mtini, whose mainstay had been the beautiful rural home where he had left a wife and two children, finally drives Nduli home, apparently cured of his illusion, the latter represented by the non-existent idealised girl of his dream, Mnandi.

> Mnandi was dead. He had been home for three days now. The sickness was leaving his body. Walking among the sheep on the hillside and among the cattle grazing in the valley, and being among his own people, away from the white man, all that had helped to take the sickness from his body. Yes, there had been great sickness in his body when he had left the city. Enough sickness to kill one man. It was all gone now. And the dream of Mnandi was gone too. It was good to be with his old mother again. To eat the food she made and listen to her voice. And it was good to be among the old men; to hear their tales of battles and glories of the past. And to go into the fields and hear the young maidens singing while they worked. All this was good. It helped to take the sickness out of his body. But why was the sickness still there in his mind? Why could not that go also? When you are with your people sickness leaves you for your people are always good to you; well, the sickness of the body had gone; why not the sickness of the mind?
>
> The old mother looked up from her corn. She saw the faraway look in his eyes.[16]

Nduli, of course, must return to the city, as he explains to his mother: 'I can only understand in the big city. There is no rest for me here. I must go back to the city.'[17] So while the people of the village put out their lights to go to bed, Nduli prepares for this journey into his own night, and into that unknown which is knowledge. The black man must return to the white man's terrain not only to emulate and learn from him but also to compete with him in order to prove himself and win acceptance as the white man's equal. Another young man, Joe, in Alex La Guma's *A Walk in the Night* explains why in spite of his abject lot he refuses to go back with his mother to the country: 'I wasn't going to the outside. To the country. Man, that would be the same like running away.'[18] Unlike the hero of Alan Paton's *Cry, the Beloved Country* who evaded the issue when he fled from the city, Nduli courageously stakes a claim for himself in the white man's world.

Nduli's dream returns to him once he reaches the city, and we are meant to conclude that its realisation is there too. He is now a son of the city, and the song of the city has become his. 'Today there is pain—but tomorrow/The song will be gay —rich with hope.'[19] The implication of Nduli's reaching the city at night is that the black man is today facing his own night in the white world, but the inevitable dawn carries within itself the promise of glory.

NOTES

[1] *Song of the City* (Dorothy Crisp and Co., London, 1943). All page references are to this edition.
[2] *Dark Testament*, p. 10.
[3] *Song of the City*, pp. 44–5.
[4] *Ibid.*, p. 45.
[5] *Tell Freedom* (Faber and Faber, London, 1954), p. 176.
[6] *Song of the City*, p. 23.
[7] *Ibid.*, p. 73.
[8] *Ibid.*, p. 77.
[9] *Ibid.*, p. 88.
[10] *Ibid.*, p. 50.
[11] *Ibid.*, pp. 133–4.
[12] *Ibid.*, p. 112.
[13] *Ibid.*, p. 103.
[14] *Ibid.*, p. 106.
[15] *Ibid.*, p. 143.
[16] *Ibid.*, p. 177.
[17] *Ibid.*, p. 178.
[18] Alex La Guma, *A Walk in the Night and Other Stories* (Heinemann, London, 1967), p. 70.
[19] *Song of the City*, p. 179.

Chapter Three

Mine Boy

Mine Boy[1] was the first South African novel written in English to attract international attention. After the ambitious attempt of *Song of the City* Abrahams seems to have realised the limitations of his capability. Xuma's story is almost a duplicate of Dick Nduli's, but Xuma is a more credible creation, precisely because Abrahams has devoted more time and effort to him. Unlike *Song of the City*, *Mine Boy* is a unified piece of work—both in conception and execution; even a strong character like Leah cannot make us forget Xuma, in spite of the considerable amount of space devoted to her. The setting is the same as in Abrahams' earlier books, the Coloured location of Vrededorp where the author himself grew up, and some of the characters who got honourable mention in *Song of the City* take the centre stage here, as in the case of Ma Plank, or Daisy, thinly disguised as Maisy. *Mine Boy* is unequivocally a city novel (it is difficult to pigeon-hole *Song of the City* so confidently), based on Marxist theory. Although *Song of the City* formally marked the break between Abrahams and the Marxists, for some time afterwards he continued to accept their dialectical interpretation of any given situation in economic terms.

Mine Boy is a situational novel, very thin on plot. This throws undue weight on character and atmosphere. Abrahams, as we have seen in *Dark Testament* and *Song of the City*, is poor on characterisation, so one of the two props of the novel is immediately knocked down. What, in fact, holds *Mine Boy* up is the simplicity with which a powerful atmosphere is created. Yet this atmosphere is one-dimensional; it all comes from the lives of the people in the slums, and our glimpses of the lives of the whites are rather fleeting and unconvincing. Abrahams does not, perhaps cannot, know the white areas as he knows intimately the slums where he spent most of his youth. Indeed, Xuma's visits to the white sections of Johannesburg are like Abrahams', very occasional, and confined to the night. Abrahams' first look at the city, like Xuma's, is at night, from a hill-top:

> I could map the city by its lights.
> That was the heart of it. There, where it was almost light as day. I could see cars and trams clearly. And the outlines of people moving. White people. To the left, and a little towards me, was Malay Camp, an inky black spot in the sea of light. Couldn't see anything there. Dark folk move in darkness; white folks move in light. Well, Malay Camp wouldn't be a slum if it were as light as the city. Slum is darkness. Dark folk live in darkness.
> Beyond Malay Camp, a little to the left again, was white Fordsburg. White: lights. Black: darkness. A strip of darkness ran through black Fordsburg and became a big black blob. Vrededorp. And to the left of it, that world of light was Mayfair. And the patch of light to the right of it was Upper, white, Vrededorp.
> To the right of me, beyond the heart of the city, lights moved away in waves. Those were the white suburbs: there was Hospital Hill; beyond it, out of sight, was Parktown and the other suburbs of light. Light is white: dark is black.[2]

Both the strength and weakness of *Mine Boy* derive from this simple interplay of colours: white and black. It is what gives resonance to the lives of the people, and the problems which confront them. The photographic method which Abrahams uses to record everything in its minutest details in an attempt to capture the essence of living in a segregated city produces a simple black–and–white picture. The opening paragraphs point out very well what to expect from the rest of the novel:

> Somewhere in the distance a clock chimed. The big man listened. One ... Two ... Three ... Three o'clock in the morning.
> He shifted the little bundle from his right hand to his left, hitched up his pants, and continued up the

39

narrow street. Full of shadows, he thought. But then this whole Malay Camp is full of shadows.

I wonder where I am, he thought. He had lost all sense of direction. Still, one street was as good as another...

And then he saw the woman at the gate. He would have passed without seeing her, for she was a part of the shadowy gate, but she coughed and moved. He went closer.[3]

Thus, Abrahams moves closer and closer to his subject. Xuma, like Dick Nduli, arrives in the city at night, but here the fact is used to achieve concrete results. In *Song of the City*, we were not able to see any of the characters. In *Mine Boy*, Abrahams goes to the other extreme, details everyone's physical make-up, so that we at least 'see' the characters, however statuesque they become in the process.

Basically, the characters are as simple as the black-and-white atmosphere in which they operate. True, Abrahams avoids the elementary fault of dividing the characters into good or bad along racial lines—Paddy O'Shea and his girlfriend, Di, are well-meaning and very good to the black population; but there are really no bad black people, for Abrahams makes their white-dominated society accountable for the failure of all the black characters. The formula which Abrahams has applied to the non-whites is quite simple: the best way to demonstrate the evil of society is to show how it has destroyed potentially noble souls.

The archetype is the derelict known to the whole of Vrededorp as 'Daddy'. In his youth he was the man all men wished to be, but in old age he becomes a moral lesson for all, a representative of thousands of young black men who come to the city to find money and life, but end in abject poverty and squalor. The lesson is very simple: the city is killing the best of black manhood. Now, 'Daddy' is an incurable alcoholic who goes mad when denied a drink, and sleeps in his own urine. The danger signal is there for everyone to read: as 'Daddy' goes so goes every black man who comes into contact with the white world—Dladla, J. P. Williamson, and the rest of them. 'Daddy' dies, appropriately from injuries sustained when he was knocked down by a motor car, a symbol of white technology and the fast pace of city living. After his death, 'Daddy' successfully obtained what he had been searching for all his life—his identity; at the head of his grave is put a little cross, with a number under which his name is written: Francis Ndabula. Each black character in *Mine Boy* needs his full name. By bestowing on each of them only one name, Abrahams wants to emphasise that individuality is denied to the blacks in South Africa, that these characters are but representatives of millions of their race. The common factor is the pathos of their lives; to all of them we can apply the formula which the author applies to Lena, a young woman beaten by life and deserted by her ambitious children: 'she knows life and she wants to forget it'.[4]

Leah, the shebeen queen, deserves more comment, if only because Abrahams has devoted so much attention to her, and still fails to make her a round character. A big, tall and strong woman she is both physically and mentally overwhelming. She disarms a man here, breaks up a street brawl there, and silences all and sundry by the force of her stare only, her head held up all the time, even as others, men and women alike, bow theirs in tearful sorrow. Yet she is not a complicated character. Xuma, on his first night in town, looks at her and comes to a judgment immediately: 'A strong woman, he decided, and those eyes can see right through a man's.'[5] Xuma's assessment is never once proved wrong. Leah represents the fiercely tough black women who operate the shebeens. Even her infrequent and fleeting moments of softness—such as her pride and lingering affection for 'my man' who was sent to jail for killing a man who tried to kiss her; or the affair she now carries on with Dladla, because 'a woman gets lonely for a plaything, that's all'; and the care she takes of Xuma, a complete stranger, as if he were her long-lost son: all are meant to illustrate how much of the original humanity of this Bantu woman has been killed by the city. But what emerges is a Dickensian figure, one-dimensional to the point of grotesqueness.

It is a measure of Abrahams' failure of characterisation that he would not expect such an unfavourable judgment of Leah, for she is held up as the one person who can fathom others. She has devised a way of coping with the city; she has even largely succeeded in mastering it, although to us she seems to have lost her soul thereby. And while we may want to blame society for brutalising such a noble woman, Abrahams himself does not see it in that light, nor does Leah, who would not plead extenuating circumstances like the other characters, especially Eliza, her step-daughter.

Leah trumpets Eliza to everyone as suffering from 'the sickness of the city'. However, Eliza, who is educated, is more articulate than anybody else in explaining what this sickness is, as she does once to Xuma her lover:

> I am no good and I cannot help myself. It will be all right if you hate me. You should beat me. But inside me there is something wrong. And it is because I want the things of the white people. I want to be like the white people and go where they go and do the things they do and I am black. I cannot help it. Inside I am not black and I do not want to be a black person. I want to be like they are, you understand, Xuma. It is no good but I cannot help it. It is just so.[6]

There is a word for Eliza's affliction—alienation; she does not belong in the white world to which she aspires because of her education, nor can she fit into the black world to which her society has condemned her because of the colour of her skin. Therefore, she is 'no good' as a human being, to use her own words. But there is really nothing else to sustain our interest in her, in spite of her beauty and her education, for both mean that her aspirations are higher than those permitted by the colour situation in her country, and thus her plaint is louder and more self-destructive.

Rather more interesting is the love triangle between Eliza, Maisy and Xuma (a parallel to the relationship between Leah, Ma Plank, and 'Daddy'), especially the contrast between Eliza's attitude to life and Maisy's. The superficial differences are rather obvious, and the novelist hammers on these—Maisy is city-bred, unschooled, and not particularly beautiful, whereas Eliza, born in the country, now has Western education and is (therefore?) a daughter of the city. The contrast goes deeper, however, and gives *Mine Boy* a greater

42

depth than we can hardly attribute to a deliberate working-out on Abrahams' part. In contrast to Eliza who is at loggerheads with her society, Maisy is subject to robust fits of laughter and makes everyone happy. There is no joyous occasion in the book at which she is not present, if indeed she is not the initiator. She has the genius for bringing out the best in Xuma, in contrast to his destructive passion for Eliza. Maisy's outlook on life can be summed up as 'joyous optimism', yet she suffers in a more profound way than any other character in the novel. She loves Xuma but is not loved in return; worse, she watches him grieving over the wayward Eliza. In 'a matter-of-fact voice', Maisy bares her heart to Xuma:

> ... speaking as though she were discussing something of no importance.
> 'To love a man who loves another is painful. Maybe it is more painful than it is to love someone who loves you and leaves you. I don't know. All I know is it is very painful to love a man who loves another. You look at him and see the light in his eyes for the other woman and your heart bleeds. You lie down to sleep and you are alone and it seems no one wants you and you think "They are together" and it hurts so that sleep will not come. And all the time you carry it in your breast. You look at them when they are together and you smile but inside you bleed. Day after day, all the time it is so. That is pain, Xuma. That is the pain I have carried for months...'[7]

Maisy is the only one who does not blame her society for her plight, although there is evidence in the story to show that she suffers from the social situation as much as anyone else. Her anguish is more typical of 'the still sad music of humanity', and has little to do with the political situation in the country. It contrasts sharply with what Xuma calls pain in his confrontation with Paddy or Eliza's complaint about the colour situation in their society. Maisy's is elemental suffering, which no social or political solutions can alleviate. She comes closest to rescuing *Mine Boy* from being just a protest novel, but then she is only a minor character.

With Xuma, the central character, we are firmly on the protest track. In every sense of the word, Xuma is a 'simple' character. He is largely a device, and the mere fact that he carries so much of the burden of the book's theme attests to Abrahams' immaturity at this point. His single name—unlike Nduli, he is given no other—robs him of all individuality, and exposes the author's intention of creating a representative figure. When we first meet him, he introduces himself, simply: 'Xuma. I come from the north.' So, here is the rustic come to town. Abrahams' intention is to shock us into an awareness of the plight of non-whites in South Africa, even as Xuma himself is shocked into an awareness of his place in the scheme of things. In spite of his huge size, he is mentally a child, but he has refused to stay in his place, for he brings the innocence of the countryside into the city, and it all looks like naïvety. The device here is comparable to having a child-hero, for at the beginning Xuma in the city is indeed like a child in the world. But Abrahams orchestrates his hero's deepening awareness meticulously, gradually opening Xuma to an ever-widening circle of shocks.

At the beginning, Xuma's life is no different from Dick Nduli's, but of course Xuma holds more possibilities. Nduli has found work as a houseboy with a white family. Abrahams has not exploited the opportunity this offered for us to see the underside of the master race—as Ferdinand Oyono does with great success in *Houseboy*—nor has he shown Nduli really learning anything from his employers. In contrast, Xuma is subjected to a barrage of 'lessons' from both 'Daddy' and Leah, surrogate parents. Leah tries assiduously to make him 'see' that country morality does not apply in the city.

> 'Listen to me Xuma from the north, you are a baby with people. I can be your mother with people. Now listen to me, maybe you will understand and maybe you will not, but listen. I like you because you are here but you are not here ... No. You don't understand ... I am here, you see, I come from my people, but I am no longer of my people. It is so in the city and I have been here many years. And this

44

city makes you strange to the ways of your people, you see?'

'Yes, yes. I see.'[8]

'Daddy' tries to drive the same lesson home with his allegory of the custom and the city:

'One day the city came to visit the custom, Xuma. And the custom was kind. It gave the city food and it gave the city beer and it gave the city beautiful young women...'

'No, Daddy,' Leah interrupted.

'Quiet, woman!' Daddy said firmly.

Leah smiled.

'... As I was saying, it gave the city beautiful young women. And then what do you think? Unbelievable. The city didn't say a word. It didn't say "No thank you" and it didn't say "Thank you". And the people said, "Ah, everything will be all right now, the custom and the city are friends." Hmmmm ... They did say that and they went out into the fields to look after their crops. And when the sun was going down they came back and looked for their beer but their beer was gone. And then they looked for the custom but he had gone too. And the city was there laughing at them. And now they go to jail if they drink beer. That's why I like beer ... Very funny, heh, Xuma?'[9]

But in spite of Leah's attempt to dragoon him into awareness and Daddy's more gentle but also more complicated explanation, Xuma does not really see or understand until he goes to the mines. Dick Nduli's job of houseboy did not fully expose him to Western influence; in contrast, mining is the man's job, it is what brings most of the young Africans from their country homes to the slums. The fact that these adults who do most of the laborious tasks are called 'boys' by their white bosses is an eloquent testimony to the white feeling of superiority vis-à-vis the Africans' lack of technological know-how. Actually, before the awesome machines, all the miners (whether white or black) are 'boys', and the machines mock their efforts; it is not the white man who is on top, but the machines which defeat the exertions of the miners even while they deceive themselves in the belief that they control the machines.

Abrahams' point is that the strongest factor which keeps the black men hopelessly tied to this demanding situation is economic. But progressively, even for the comparatively inarticulate Xuma, it becomes difficult to stick to a purely economic reading of the situation. By entering the mines Xuma enters the white man's world, and even he notices before long that the graduations are based on colour. Abrahams has written elsewhere: 'Every white miner is a "boss". By law the Blacks are forbidden to do skilled work or get the wages of a skilled miner. A skilled miner is one who has a White face. When a White miner does a drilling job it becomes a skilled job. When a Black miner does it it is unskilled.'[10] Abrahams tries in *Mine Boy* to dampen these overtly racial overtones. First, Xuma is unpoliticised, interested only in his work; and because he cannot or does not articulate his racial awareness, he is 'the good native' to the whites. Furthermore, Paddy O'Shea, Xuma's boss, is introduced to complicate Xuma's awareness, for at least here is one white man who offers friendship.

The story becomes overtly ideological when Paddy enters. His nickname, the 'Red One', is enough to brand him a Marxist, and he has the characteristics of all of Abrahams' communist characters—well-meaning and earnest, but hard, brooding, and joyless. To Xuma he says: 'Don't call me boss,'[11] but obviously can't bring himself to say the rest: Call me comrade. None the less, he does his best to convince Xuma that they share the same cause:

> The moon was far to the west. The stars could hardly be seen. And the black man and the white were like two men alone in the world. There was no other sign of life around them. In the distance they could see the mine dumps towering against the sky, and in the opposite direction they could see the tall buildings of Johannesburg. There was a hush in the cool morning air. It was as though the world held its breath.

46

'You say you understand,' Xuma said, 'but how can you? You are a white man. You do not carry a pass. You do not know how it feels to be stopped by a policeman in the street. You go where you like. You do not know how it feels when they say "Get out! White people only." Did your woman leave you because she is mad with wanting the same things the white man has? Did you know Leah? Did you love her? Do you know how it feels to see her go to jail for nine months? Do you know Leah's house? Did Leah take you in in the middle of the night?' Xuma's voice rose. 'Did Leah talk to you and laugh with you from the side of her mouth? You say you understand. Did you feel these things like I do? How can you understand, white man! You understand with your head. I understand with pain. With the pain of my heart. That is understanding, not just the head and lips. I feel things! You want me to be your friend. How can I be your friend when your people do this to me and my people?'

'What you say is true, Zuma, these things have not happened to me so I do not feel them, but tell me this. Do you think a black man can feel them if they did not happen to him? Has Johannes got the same feeling about Leah, about Eliza? He did not love Eliza. Maybe he's sorry for you because you are his friend. But can he feel like you did about Eliza? Tell me.'

'Johannes is black like me and he knows Eliza left me because of the white man, he knows Leah is in jail because of that. When he is sober there is great unhappiness in his heart because he knows these things.'

'There is always great unhappiness in my heart.'

'You are white.'

'I am a man first. I want you to be a man first and then a black man.'

'I am a black man. My people are black. I love them.'

'That is good. It is good to love one's people and

not to be ashamed of what one is. But it is not good to think only as a black man or only as a white man. The white people in this country think only as white people and that is why they do this harm to your people.'

'Then I must think as a black man.'

'No. You must think as a man first. You must be a man first and then a black man. And if it is so you will understand as a black man and also as a white man. That is the right way, Zuma. When you understand that you will be a man with freedom inside your breast. It is only those who are free inside who can help those around them.'

Xuma shook his head and stared away to the east. The first rays of the morning sun were showing against the sky.[12]

Against the background of the towering mine-dumps on one hand and the skyscrapers on the other (both as emblems of the white man's achievement and the black man's deprivation), this dawn dialogue between boss and boy, white and black, significantly ends on a note of mutual understanding and respect. The new day—the most persistent symbol in Abrahams' writing—has been long in coming, and in terms of Abrahams' vision of the future of the plural societies it is a day to which all the races should contribute something. Earlier, the O'Sheas, by inviting Xuma to their house, had given him his first opportunity of being on intimate terms with whites. What he had not understood from his visit to the O'Sheas he later learnt from Dr Mini, a middle-class black, who did not shy from pushing everyone around in his line of duty, and had scared a bullying white policeman. Abrahams' uncritical portrayal of the O'Sheas and Dr Mini indicates that he is more interested in the message than in the agents. His intention is that Xuma should free himself from the white people's image of him, learn not to accept the inferior position to which the white rulers of the country have thrust every black man. His aim is to make Xuma a man instead of a boy, an articulate spokesman for his race, instead of being the white man's good native.

Xuma's progress from boyhood to manhood is made a part of his growth into a full human being. But Abrahams goes a step further by making the whole process of Xuma's becoming a full human being synonymous with his becoming a Westernised African, as close to the white man as his black skin will allow. For Abrahams, Westernisation holds the key for the future development of the black man, and the way is to develop an individual personality. So Xuma moves closer to the whites both in thought and appearance. Although he shuns patronisation by rejecting 'kindness', yet it is the black man who has to learn from his white brother or comrade—Paddy can teach Xuma to 'understand', but Xuma has nothing to teach his boss. However, they part as friends and equals, although each pursues his own way, for now there is common understanding.

Xuma's new awareness is like a new wine, it gets into his head, and he recreates the world in a new image, a world in which colour would not be important and where human beings would be judged as individuals—and where all individuals would be happy. Life in South Africa is a negation of this noblest aspiration. Immediately Xuma wakes up, sober after his intoxicating dream, his empty stomach shows how far his world is from the ideal. Most of what we know about Xuma up to this point has been through his actions, and through the comments of others; but now, to bring out Xuma's deepening perception, Abrahams thrusts us deeply into his character's thoughts by a skilful use of interior monologue:

> Reaction set in. He felt alone and bitter and unhappy. The world was a dark place. Darker than it had ever been. Before he had been unhappy and lonely but not like this. Before his unhappiness had been only feeling. Now he had something against which to set his pain and unhappiness and it made it greater. It made it too big for him to bear. It pressed in on him and hot waves of pain and hatred rose in his breast and made his eyes burn. Yes! He hated all white people and he hated the Red One. If the Red One had not spoken to him it would not have been

so now. But hatred did not ease the tightness round his head. It made it worse. He wanted something that would take that tightness away. To feel as he did before the Red One had spoken to him, just empty and without so much feeling, even that would be better than feeling as he did now.[13]

Xuma's bitterness is psychologically valid; the original security of his innocence has been pierced and the world suddenly becomes an unsafe place. Anger and hatred are not sufficient, for Xuma needs something positive, an action that would be a blow to the oppressive system and at the same time an expression of his new-found dignity. His opportunity comes with the death of his friend, J. P. Williamson, killed by a collapsing mine roof, an accident that could have been prevented if the white engineer had paid attention to the warnings of both Xuma and Paddy. Williamson and his white boss were killed as they kept the roof up with their bodies in order to enable the other miners to escape. This sacrificial death by two men of different colours in order to save people, irrespective of their colour, finally convinces Xuma of the way he ought to go. Defiantly he calls on the other miners to rally round him in a boycott of the mines until conditions are made safer.

> Xuma felt good suddenly. Strong and free. A man.
> 'We are men!' he shouted. 'It does not matter if our skins are black! We are not cattle to throw away our lives! We are men!'
> 'This is a strike,' the manager cried. He pointed at Xuma and shouted: 'You will go to jail! I have called the police! They will be here soon!'
> 'We will not go down if you say so, Xuma!' a man shouted.
> Xuma felt stronger than he had ever felt in all his life. Strong enough to be a man without colour. And now, suddenly, he knew that it could be so. Man could be without colour.
> 'Build up the place and we will go down!' he shouted. 'Build it up properly. Johannes was my

friend! He was our friend! Now he is dead! Build up the place!'

'Those who are not striking come on this side!' the manager shouted and stepped to the left. All the indunas and the white men moved over to the left.

Only Paddy remained where he was. Xuma and the mine boys were on the right, the manager and the indunas and the other white men on the left. Paddy was in the centre.

'O'Shea!' the manager called.

It seemed that Paddy did not hear him.

'Come on, Paddy!' a white man called. 'It's all very well to play with them sometimes but we must show these kaffirs where they belong. Come on!'

This is what I argued with Di about, Paddy thought. This is the test of all my verbal beliefs. Zuma has taken the leadership, I must follow. Di was wrong about him. He's a man.

In the distance they could hear the siren of the police cars. Soon now the police would be there.

Paddy walked over to Xuma and took his hand.

'I am a man first, Xuma,' he said. Then he turned to the other mine boys and shouted: 'Xuma is right! They pay you a little! They don't care if you risk your lives! Why is it so? Is not the blood of a black man red like that of a white man? Does not a black man feel too? Does not a black man love life too? I am with you! Let them fix up the place first!'

Xuma smiled. Now he understood. He understood many things. One can be a person first. A man first and then a black man or a white man...[14]

The battle line has been re-drawn, not to pitch black against white, but the exploited black miners against their white bosses and the black indunas. Even Paddy has passed the final test on which so many liberal whites had fallen—he readily accepts black leadership.

Xuma's fear, which makes him run away from police brutality, only confirms his new-won humanity, for there can be no courage without fear, and fear comes only from imagination. He gains in stature and more than redeems himself when he decides to surrender to the police. This is true courage, for he has conquered fear itself, even the greatest fear—fear of the unknown. Resolutely he is determined to face the worst cruelty of the South African police. He is at the end a nobler and stronger person than he had ever been at any time in his life. At the end Xuma is articulate and confident enough to feel that he can be the spokesman for the black cause, a long way from the dumb man who reached the city several months ago. 'It is only those who are free inside who can help free those around them.'[15]

However, Abrahams knows that the end is not yet in sight, for ahead lie suffering and sadness not only for Xuma but also for his country. This is the significance of that quiet ending, a deceptive quietness when contrasted with the turbulence of the story. The other blacks continue in that darkness from which Xuma has emerged, human and dignified, as a result of his exposure to the white world:

> One by one the lights of Malay Camp were turned out. One by one the lights of Vrededorp and the other dark places of Johannesburg, of South Africa were turned out.
>
> The streets were empty. The leaning, tired houses were quiet. Only shadows moved everywhere. Only the quiet hum of the night hung over the city. Over Vrededorp. Over Malay Camp.[16]

NOTES

[1] *Mine Boy* (Faber and Faber, London, 1946). All page references are to this edition.
[2] *Tell Freedom*, pp. 204–5.
[3] *Mine Boy*, p. 11.
[4] *Ibid.*, p. 9.
[5] *Ibid.*, p. 13.
[6] *Ibid.*, p. 89.
[7] *Ibid.*, p. 225.
[8] *Ibid.*, p. 23.
[9] *Ibid.*, p. 25.
[10] *Return to Goli*, p. 101.
[11] *Mine Boy*, p. 72.
[12] *Ibid.*, pp. 236–7.
[13] *Ibid.*, pp. 241–2.
[14] *Ibid.*, pp. 247–9.
[15] *Ibid.*, p. 237.
[16] *Ibid.*, p. 252.

Chapter Four

The Path of Thunder

The Path of Thunder was published first in America[1] before it was published in England[2] almost certainly because it was felt that a book about interracial love would receive more attention in the United States than in Britain. It was widely reviewed and extravagantly lauded in both countries. The novel is a failure, one may admit from the outset, but it is a failure for which Abrahams' earlier books have prepared us, and its major weaknesses have very little to do with the theme itself, except in so far as any South African writer who examines interracial love must follow the government's example, take sex out of the bedroom and put it on the pages of the newspapers. The notes of special pleading which the 'authorial' character Mako spreads throughout the novel under the guise of discussion with his friends—Isaac the Jew, Lanny the Coloured, both are carefully chosen by the author—are bad enough. But either through impatience at having to use even such a thinly disguised mask or because the occasion does not permit anybody but the author to be present, we get in addition a thick overlay of authorial pleading. Below is the account of Lanny and Sarie having sex for the first time:

> They got off and walked some distance, holding hands. And the moon was high and the night enchanted. A time for love. They sank to the warm, welcoming earth, and under the stars and the moon on the soft grass in the open they said with their bodies what was too deep and strong for human language.
>
> And as she lay spent and uplifted in his arms she whispered:
>
> 'I feel holy, Lanny.'
>
> And he whispered:

'Love is holy, my dear.'

'Beautiful and holy,' she murmured and closed her eyes.

... O earth! Tell thy stupid children to love. Tell them for they are in need of telling. In need of the simple things. In need of sympathy and understanding and brotherliness. In need of a love stronger and bigger than country and race, a love that embraces all countries and all races, the ultimate love of man for man. And teach them too, O earth, an anger, just and righteous, that offers peace only to men of good will. Tell them all hearts are sacred, all hearts can ache ... Tell them ... Tell them while one man and one woman cannot love in safety there is security for none ... Tell them ...[3]

The author has broken his own injunction, tried to verbalise 'what was too deep and strong for human language', and collapsed on a ridiculously pathetic note. Pleadings such as this run throughout *The Path of Thunder* leading to the book's melodramatic end when Lanny and Sarie, barricaded in her house, defy the agents of hatred and shoot it out to the bitter end.

Lanny Swartz and Sarie Villier, the first of Abrahams' heroes, possess those qualities which the novelist considers most important in a plural society—freedom of the heart from fear and hatred. We have the author's assurance that Lanny's generosity of mind extends to his oppressors. 'He didn't hate anything. He didn't hate the whites. Only in short spells, when they did him any harm, did he feel bitter. But it passed away and he didn't want to fight anybody.' Apparently, Lanny is that man whom everyone in combat against apartheid should wish to be. Using his love for a white girl as his only weapon, he defies the might of his society. 'The love that is between him and that girl has made him human. The inhibitions caused by oppression have left him.'

In *Dark Testament* Western education was the panacea which turned the nigger into a full human being. In *The Path of Thunder* Abrahams moves a step further. The point is that Lanny in spite of his Western education (he has a BA and has

54

won scholarships) is still less than a human being, and only the love of Sarie opens to him life on the highest plane, because this is the plane on which the mind takes hold of and conquers fear. 'There is something like inevitability about the way they seem drawn to each other. They don't seem to be able to control their feelings.'⁶ Even the fatality that surrounds their love is a defiance of the South African laws which attempt to regulate human emotions. Interracial love humanises the couple because it enables them to burst the shackles of oppression put on them by the colour bar; it is the only antidote to fear and hatred, the principal wares of South African life. For example, it is only after confessing her love for Lanny that Sarie feels free to visit Tante, a visit which had been forbidden by Gert Villier.

Fear in various forms runs through *The Path of Thunder*; all the characters are haunted by it almost to the point of paralysis. Mako gives way to fear when he counsels Lanny to run away:

> You see, you cannot protect your love and keep the outside world away all the time. You live in the world and the world is going to find you out. And because it is a stupid, mad world, this in which we live, it is going to hurt you and your love and your woman. Perhaps in other lands, though they are very few, where colour is not a crime, you would have been happy. Here you cannot be.
>
> Do this for your people, for the future. Go away from here, live in another place and fight till your people are no longer slaves so that one day in the future if another Coloured man loves another white woman they will be free to love openly and it will not be a crime. That is a good thing to do for your people.
>
> And in the fight you will find forgetfulness and your pain will be less. You see, Swartz, you and I, our generation, are born to the fight, my friend. For us there is no time for love. There is only the fight to live and be men instead of slaves. We must leave the quiet song in the evening. It is not for us to stop and

listen and be soft. Our hearts must be hard. If they
are not we die, though we be alive. And those who
come after us too.

We must fight for a time when the sun will shine
and the birds will sing and the hearts of our people
will be brighter than the sun and the song of their
hearts will be gayer and louder than that of the birds.
We must fight for that time. We must go forward
and fight, my brother, because for us there can be no
rest. Come then, my brother, will you go away?[7]

In spite of the tones of militancy in which Mako's plea is
couched, his is a counsel to submit to fear and despair. Here is
the germ of a theme which recurs again and again in
Abrahams' novels, the view of South Africa as a moral wilderness where it is an act of weakness to submit to humane
feelings. In order to win, it is necessary to be hard, as Leah
seemed to have demonstrated in *Mine Boy*, and to suppress all
humanity. Above all, it is a situation which feeds the impulse
towards group identity. All the attempts to make Lanny see
reason either by Fieta or by Mako are counsels to save his own
skin or place the interests of his people above everything else.
Oppression intensifies the herd instinct, and so does a state of
war, but interracial love symbolises a union stronger than any
group identity such as tribalism or nationalism. Lanny's
original duty is to his community, the Coloured people of
Stilleveld, for whom he plans to open a school; his title of 'the
returning son' emphasises this role as the symbol of group
aspirations. He transcends this narrow label when he puts
aside personal safety, even the immediate interests of his
people, and fights for all humanity by asserting his right to
love a white girl. It is left to another character who had been
tnrough fire to spell out what it means:

Sam touched his face with his sound hand. The left
side of his face twisted upward. Deep wisdom
showed in his eyes. Fieta turned away. It was impossible to keep looking at Sam when he had that
light in his eyes. It was like looking at God if there
was a God.

'You can't stop it, Fieta,' he said in a faraway

voice. 'You see, love is strong. Stronger than hate even. Love is the only thing that can kill hate, nothing else. You see, hate destroys and that's why love is stronger. It builds. There is hope for all Coloured people in this country, while one white woman can love one Coloured man. Love keeps one alive. It makes you understand and fight... Look at me, Fieta.'[8]

But when we look at Sam we see a human wreck ('a thing', as he is gloatingly referred to by the sadistic white man who had brutalised him thirty years ago), treated with unwonted kindness by the rest of his people, an object of pity to all, the remains of the once physically strong and handsome Samuel DuPlessis. Mad Sam's story provides a sub-plot to the main story, a forwarning of the fate that awaits Lanny and all those who assault the South African racial barrier. But it does more. Abrahams' theme is not death, but life, not the destructive realities of hatred, but the resurrecting potentialities of love. Sam had been almost done to death by Gert Villier's hatred, but the unflinching devotion and love of Fieta has kept him alive and human by providing the only focal point of sanity in his disordered world.

The other characters, without being physically deformed like Mad Sam, do not come alive even for one moment. Gert Villier, the local white *baas*, represents Abrahams' picture of the Afrikaner, incurably opposed to change and progress. Up on the hill, Gert is the figure of the archvillain, breathing heavily and deliberately, a Dickensian figure with his 'big hands pressed down on the table, his huge body relaxed and impersonal'.[9] Mako the native gets more attention from the author, deliberately, for he is fashioned as a mouthpiece. Like all of Abrahams' surrogates, he is slender and small-boned, detached and thoughtful; and besides his profession as a school teacher, he is indeed an artist, for he reveals himself as a poet:

What is the good of names? ... For me, I pray for the beautiful things. I like the beautiful things, the free things and the free people. I try to dig past the names to find the good and beautiful. Maybe one day all the

57

world will want to do so too. It wants to now, but
maybe it doesn't know it.[10]

Mako's one-man audience here is Isaac Finkelberg the Jew
who had attended college in the city, which explains his
admiration for both Lanny and Sarie, although his common
sense opposes the relationship:

> It was a break with tradition and convention and the
> racial nonsense of the past. It was a revolt against
> nationalist tyranny, an assertion of the basic fact that
> a person was a person irrespective of colour ...
> living on the highest plane, love like this, free of
> nationalities and racialism.[3]

The point of meeting between Mako and Isaac is really not
the tedious evening seminars where they analyse race, nation,
and nationalism—although Abrahams uses these sessions to
keep us informed of his own standpoint on these issues—but
that they are both young, and not afraid to take issue with their
elders. Abrahams' optimistic point that hope lies in the children derives from the poem, *Tableau*, by the black American
poet Countee Cullen, from which he has taken the title of his
book:

> Locked arm in arm they cross the way
> The black boy and the white,
> The golden splendour of the day,
> The sable pride of night.
>
> From lowered blinds the dark folk stare,
> And here the fair folk talk,
> Indignant that these two should dare
> In unison walk.
>
> Oblivious to look and word
> They pass, and see no wonder
> That lighting brilliant as a sword
> Should blaze the path of thunder.[12]

Abrahams, true to his source, allows the youths to occupy
the stage while their elders—Lanny's mother, the old coloured

preacher, old Mr Finkelberg—battle ineffectually with their offsprings and with time. This is a young man's book, and the problems are those of youth: passion and its dangers. The adults seem tamed by time; like Mr Finkelberg they think they have found 'peace' in their old age, but what they have cultivated is resignation. When, finally, thunder strikes, the difference in the attitudes of the two generations is remarkable:

Down in Stilleveld the coloured community gathered fearfully in a bunch and listened to the shots that rent the air. No one knew what it was all about till Fieta came, carrying the body of Mad Sam down the High Street. And above the sound of their voices, questioning, carried the voices of the guns.

With Fieta was the young Jew Isaac and the black man Mako. Fieta carried Sam into her mother's house and laid him gently on the bed. Her eyes were bitter and hard. The people crowded into the little room.

'It is Lanny Swartz,' Fieta said bitterly. 'He and Sarie Villier are in love. They were running away. They're up there, fighting.'

Sister Swartz collapsed in a heap. The rest were stunned into paralysed silence.

The preacher went down on his knees. The others followed him. Only young Mako and Isaac and Fieta remained standing ... Above the silence carried the voices of the guns ... The voice of Mako mingled with the voices of the guns.

'They loved. That is all they did ... They harmed no one. They were drawn together because they were people of a kind ... Two young people of a kind ... And now there are the guns ... This is indeed slavery ... It is not enough to go on your knees, preacher, and call to your God ... Listen to the guns ... Up there they are fighting side by side because it is a crime to love ... We must *do* something ... What are we to do?'[13]

Such a *denouement* confirms Abrahams' moral earnestness, and further weakens *The Path of Thunder* as a work of art: it is not the duty of the artist, but that of the propagandist, to suggest solutions to social problems. In a glowing review, *The Times Literary Supplement* praised Abrahams for demonstrating in this novel 'the skill of a practised writer' and pronounced the book a work of art rather than a tract: 'His book is ... not a tract and it offers neither analysis nor solution to the problems of educating the coloured African. It contains the blunt, brutal facts in dramatic terms, and it is impossible not to be moved by them.'[14] However, the voice that is challenging 'the voices of the guns' is once again Mako's, but of course it is also Abrahams'. The dilemma posed by the last question is very real, no less than Abrahams' not-so-subtle suggestion of a way out. What are we to do? The answer is simple: Do as the young ones are doing, who refuse to bow down on their knees in prayer, but instead mingle their own voices with the voices of the guns. Above all, do as those two youths, Lanny and Sarie, are doing, who die fighting side by side in defence of love.

The female characters are better drawn than their male counterparts, both individually and collectively. There is more individuality here which means more than just the physical differences noticeable among the men. In spite of their difference, the women seem to understand one another, sharing what we may call a feminine attitude to life, something missing among the men. The most interesting character in the novel, if not the most subtly portrayed, is Fieta. Her type is fairly firmly established—Daisy in *Song of the City* and Maisy in *Mine Boy*, from whom she got her voluptuous figure, happy disposition, as well as her easy morality. Fieta takes a hand in straightening everybody's problems. We see her in one moment reclaiming the insane Sam, in another arranging a meeting between Sarie and Celia, Lanny's city-bred Coloured girlfriend from the Cape. As in the case of Mabel, Lanny's sister, whose world has come to an end because her lover has left her, Fieta gives everybody a chance to find a new life, or at least to pick up the shattered remains of the old one.

Mabel's story of love and its loss serves as another sub-plot (the number of sub-plots makes the novel read like a collection of short stories) to her brother's main story. Not that Mabel is new; she is Eliza of *Mine Boy* put on the veld. She moans: 'I want beautiful clothes and shoes and I want to go places and meet people—young men who are nice.'[15] We detect the influence of Fieta here; and, like Fieta, Mabel has run away from home to fulfil her ambition. But the whole story is too long-drawn out, for a script which we know could have no surprises, even to the tragic finale. Abrahams' lack of economy obscures the essential significance of Mabel's story, her growth into adulthood. Mabel, physically matured but mentally a child before her brief love affair began, has at last become a part of her harsh surroundings; her personal suffering has integrated her into her world, so full of suffering. Reading her story we remember the definition of tragedy given by the hero of Chinua Achebe's *No Longer At Ease*: 'Real tragedy is never resolved. It goes on hopelessly. Conventional tragedy is too easy. The hero dies and we feel a purging of the emotions. A real tragedy takes place in a corner, in an untidy spot. The rest of the world is unaware of it.'[16] Mabel doesn't know, but we know, and even her mother and brother know, that there is no hiding place in South Africa from the colour situation.

Perhaps the best way to measure the failure of *The Path of Thunder* is to say that Abrahams conceived of the novel as a tragedy. Mako never allows us to forget how tragic the situation is:

> The tragedy is not in Swartz and this girl. The tragedy is in this land and in our time. You must be first a native or a half-caste or a Jew or an Arab or an Englishman or a Chinese or a Greek, that is the tragedy. You cannot be a human being first. That is the crime of our time.[17]

The situation between Lanny and Sarie has tragic potentialities but they are unrealised, because it is impossible to make a tragic hero of a puppet. Lanny is too mechanical to be a full human being, although we may partly blame—as he does—the situation for his predicament; it is fear, according to him, which parches his throat and renders him both physically

61

and emotionally impotent. So, when Abrahams, or Mako, says that the tragedy is not in Swartz or Sarie he is being unwittingly correct, or at least partly so. For it is Sarie who rescues the novel, just as she saves Lanny and breathes into him whatever whiff of life he has at the end.

Sarie is too complicated to be easily pigeon-holed, too firmly rooted on earth to dwell permanently in the clouds. We are enthralled with the simplicity with which she defeats Celia Richards, Lanny's city-bred fiancée from Cape Town, who comes to Stilleveld to claim her own; in other circumstances it would have been a no-contest, with the advantages weighing heavily on Celia's side—the same colour as Lanny, also more beautiful than Sarie, more educated and more sophisticated. Yet Sarie unwittingly turns all these disadvantages to her favour.

But how could Lanny love this squat peasant girl? Celia asked herself. That isn't true, she thought. The girl isn't beautiful but she's not a squat peasant girl. That was only a bit of the cat.

'Well?' Sarie repeated.

Celia noticed the quiet assurance in her voice. She found a cigarette and lit it. I must be calm with this girl, she decided.

'I came to see you about Lanny.'

'I thought so.'

'I want you to leave him alone.'

'For you?' Sarie asked softly.

Celia bit her lower lip and looked away. The girl's soft voice was getting on her nerves.

'No. Not for me but because nothing could ever come of it. You are white, but he's Coloured. Nothing can ever come of it. There are lots of white men from whom you could have chosen. Why did you have to choose him? Leave him alone for his own sake.'

'I didn't choose him,' Sarie said slowly.

'Let's not beat about the bush,' she said sharply.

'I didn't choose him,' Sarie repeated.

'A woman sees a man,' Celia said bluntly. 'She

likes what she sees and makes up her mind. That's what you did. That's what we all do. Later on, in the course of time we fall in love. Only cheap novelists and romantic idiots believe in love at first sight.'

Sarie smiled. A quiet private smile.

'What I said is true. You may believe it or not, just as you like. Things just happened.'

'And what about Lanny?'

'It was the same,' Sarie said slowly. She was getting a little tired of the cleverness of this beautiful girl from Cape Town. 'He tried to fight it, just as I did, but it was not good. But of course, you are too wise to understand that; it's too simple, a boy and a girl meeting each other and loving.'

'But you are white!' Celia accused.

With an effort Sarie controlled her mounting anger. You must understand that this girl is hurt, Sarie, she told herself. It eased her.

'I'm a woman,' she said kindly.

'He loved me,' Celia said desperately.

Sarie controlled the impulse to tell her to find another man and make up her mind about it, as she had with Lanny.[18]

The greater test is yet to come, but we know she will win that too, for hers is not a destructive love. We knew this even before she discovered her passion for Lanny, when she and her dog unwittingly arrived on the scene just as Gert was about to crush Lanny, as he had crushed Samuel DuPlessis, and the assailant fled before the dog. Sarie then invited Lanny to her house to wash the blood from his mouth and dust off his coat. This was the beginning of their love. And throughout, the emphasis is on what she does for Lanny, the extra dimension which she gives to his life, by making a full human being out of him, soothing the tensions that race hatred had injected into the nature of all the oppressed. Sarie had herself not been free of colour prejudice as was evidenced at their first meeting when she found Lanny too forward for a Coloured. The unstated assumption here is significant. However, Abrahams drops this, and emphasises that there is in fact something in

63

Sarie's nature that is fundamentally against colour discrimination. 'There was something calm and quiet that flowed from her. Flowed into him and eased and rested him. Made him want to lay his head on her lap and go to sleep. Made him forget that she was white and he was Coloured. Made him feel like a man.'[19] Sarie is able to perform this function because she herself has made the transition from being a white woman to just being a woman. She is not conscious of Lanny's colour: 'she swept race and colour and nationality away as though it were a filthy little cobweb'.[20]

The prospect of running away to Portuguese East Africa with her man brings out the contrast between Sarie's open nature and the closed surroundings in which she lives:

> In her heart was a song. She was going with her man. Away from all this hate and bitterness. And they would walk together in public and be normal and happy and free. No hiding. No fear that someone might find out and harm Lanny. Everything was going to be all right. And she would be able to look after him. Wash his clothes, mend his socks, see to his food, and keep his home clean and happy. And on Sundays they would lie in the sun and listen to the birds. And of an evening they would walk in the lighted streets without being afraid of being seen. And suddenly it dawned on her how much fear there had been in their lives. Whether they had known it or not, fear had controlled and dominated them. It had made them shun the paths trod by other men. It had made them seek quiet, secret places where they could share their love in safety.
>
> Soon all that would be over. Their love would come out into the open daylight and sunshine and no man would be able to harm it. It would be right and normal and natural. Free.[21]

Of course it is not to be. But the prospect itself illustrates well enough how Abrahams could, had he wanted, have written a Hollywood-style love story with a happy ending where Lanny and Sarie—praise be to God Almighty, free at last!—would lie in the sun and live happily ever after. The 'right and normal and natural' could happen, but not often in South Africa. With a firm grip of reality, Abrahams makes the story end unhappily. For his generation, not the fulfilment but the struggle.

When at last the two lovers are surprised and their escape frustrated, Sarie's thoughts—we are never allowed into Lanny's at this critical point in his life—are for her lover, and his safety. 'They must not hurt Lanny! The thought shot through her mind and banished all her fears. She would fight for him, do anything for him.'[22] She does all that is necessary under the circumstances—fights with him, and dies with him, for love. What greater love is there, than that an Afrikaner girl should lay down her life for her Coloured man? The two lovers' courage, which had already ignited the youths of Stille-veld, contrasts with the cowardice with which the white press reports the incident in the closing words of the novel:

> The Eastern Post of the next day carried a story on its front page in bold black letters. It told how a young Coloured teacher, one Lanny Swartz, had run amok, killed a prominent farmer, Mr Gert Villier, and then been chased into the house of Mr Villier.
>
> Alone in the house was Miss Sarie Villier. He had found a gun, shot her, and then turned the gun on his pursuers. In the ensuing battle three other people had been killed before Swartz had finally been shot down.
>
> The story ended with a strong protest against educating black people.[23]

The Path of Thunder ends as a strong protest novel whose didacticism is never far below the surface. For instance, the white newspaper moral drawn from the incident is meant to be balanced by what Mako, the author's mouthpiece, says is the real moral: 'This love of theirs is a symbol of man's attempt to move beyond the chains that bind him. For them there is nothing in it. For others there will be a lesson in it, and the lesson will be very big.' Abrahams' indignation with the whites in South Africa, as he states clearly in virtually all his non-fictional writing, is that they have closed their hearts to change, and lost the capacity to learn to adapt. The indictment is rather muted here, especially when compared with the novels written after his visit to South Africa when he saw how much conditions had worsened since he left in 1939.

The Path of Thunder, in spite of the holocaust with which it closes, is open to the future. On the eve of their first meeting, Isaac had entered, somewhat ominously, in his diary: 'Something is going to happen here soon. I wonder what. A village in Africa. It sounds very good. It sounds human and friendly. A Jew, a halfcaste, and a negro are meeting tonight in a village in Africa.'[25] But the chronicler himself could not have foreseen the holocaust that would come out of a chance meeting between a white girl and a Coloured man. For at the end it becomes necessary for the youths to stand up and answer the call of the guns, instead of just meeting to discuss the problems of South Africa. When finally the sound and the fury is over, the number of casualties is high: at least six people. But even within the holocaust Abrahams detects a new beginning. As the title of the book indicates, many people will be blighted for daring to stand in the path of thunder, but, intones Mako, 'after the storm, the earth is wet and fresh, the old rotten trees are down. There must be a new sowing, new planting, and the new maize and the new trees must be nursed. So it is with the earth and so with the minds of men.'[26] Once again, Abrahams, by rooting his faith in the natural order, makes its realisation truly inevitable.

NOTES

[1] *The Path of Thunder* (Harper, New York, 1948).
[2] *The Path of Thunder* (Faber and Faber, London, 1952). All page references are to this edition.
[3] *Ibid.*, pp. 246–7.
[4] *Ibid.*, p. 130.
[5] *Ibid.*, p. 227.
[6] *Ibid.*, p. 162.
[7] *Ibid.*, pp. 220–1.
[8] *Ibid.*, pp. 169–70.
[9] *Ibid.*, p. 68.
[10] *Ibid.*, p. 95.
[11] *Ibid.*, p. 219.
[12] *Contributions in Afro-American and African Studies* (Greenwood Publishing, New York, 1971).
[13] *The Path of Thunder*, pp. 260–1.
[14] *The Times Literary Supplement*, March 21, 1952, p. 201.
[15] *Ibid.*, p. 100.

[16] Chinua Achebe, *No Longer at Ease* (Heinemann, London, 1960), p. 39.

[17] *The Path of Thunder*, p. 227.
[18] *Ibid.*, pp. 213–4.
[19] *Ibid.*, p. 157.
[20] *Ibid.*, p. 163.
[21] *Ibid.*, p. 245.

[22] *Ibid.*, p. 256.
[23] *Ibid.*, p. 262.
[24] *Ibid.*, pp. 22–3.
[25] *Ibid.*, p. 80.
[26] *Ibid.*, p. 229.

Chapter Five

Wild Conquest

Wild Conquest[1] is Abrahams' best novel. Here the artist and the historian fuse into one. Abrahams had always been interested in history, but here he writes about the past as a means of writing about the present, shows that what has been is closely intertwined with what might have been, that not only the present realities but also the future possibilities are rooted in past experience. The conception of *Wild Conquest* is grand, truly epic, although the execution is flawed. By taking us to the beginning of the conflict within his plural society Abrahams attempts to see the whole problem with 'the long eye of history', and to fit the problems of the different groups into general human pattern.

In spite of its tripartite division (common in Abrahams' novels), *Wild Conquest* is more unified organically than the other novels; a remarkable achievement, considering the diversity of the material here. Book one derives its title, *Bible and Rifle*, from a favourite saying of a leader of the Boers: 'With my rifle and my Bible I fear no man, I fear no beast, I fear no spirit.'[2] The Boers have always considered themselves as the new children of Israel, led by God through the wilderness; trekking thus becomes more than a peculiar response to a particular problem—how to cope with encroaching British influence—but a way of life. The title of Book Two, *Bayete!* the royal salute of the Matabele, the dominant African tribe with which the Boers come into conflict, also describes a way of life, for the life of the empire is centred round the king. Book Three titled *New Day*, brings the resolution of the conflict between these two ways of life; for the defeated Matabele as well as their jubilating conquerors, it is the end of the old order and the beginning of a new one. It is a new day, for better or for worse.

Abrahams' angle of narration changes with his subject. In Book One, he looks northwards with the trekkers; in Book

Two, he looks southwards as the Matabele begin to feel the pressure from the advancing Boers; in Book Three, he stands above the conflict, and takes an objective perspective of the happenings. Considering the novel as a whole, Abrahams fits the action into the universal scheme of things. His preface to the novel has the quality and the function of the Book of Genesis in the Bible:

> Poised in space, held between nothing and nothing, there floats a golden ball. Not only is it golden. It is blue as well, and red and green, and brown, and grey. Touch gold and blue and red and green and brown and grey—touch them with love and there is poetry.
>
> Such is our earth.
>
> And high, very high up in the mountains an old man broods over the earth. For want of knowledge we call him Wind. Eternally he sits up there and sighs and whispers, and, eternally from age to age we hear his whisper and do not understand.
>
> When the moon passes and the beasts are asleep, he whispers. Sometimes softly, sometimes loudly, but he whispers. When the brightest and best of the stars of the morning come out, he whispers, tenderly. When noonday sits high in the sky, he whispers in a voice almost beyond the reach of hearing.
>
> The mountains respond to his whisper. The valleys pick up the echoes. The swaying grass-blades dance to its music. The brown-grey earth rolls over to listen. And the sky, the peerless sky, is partner with the whispering old man.
>
> Only man is on the outside, alone and out of touch, not a part of this preconceived, pre-planned order. Only man, poised between nothing and nothing, is the equal of the golden ball. Only man, between darkness and darkness, knows not the meaning of the whispering voice. So, only man is alone, haunted by fear and the echoes that flow from fear.
>
> The golden ball, which is the earth, which is

poetry and love, looks on while man grapples with
his fear.

The old man whispers the answer...[3]

Abrahams has here, with an almost unsurpassable skill, set the
scene for the conflicts that will follow. The earth is a beautiful
place where everything is integrated—except man; there is,
indeed, an interlocked relationship between the universe and
its Creator, for his spirit informs all things—except man. The
repetition of 'only man' in the penultimate paragraph is particularly forceful in setting off the alienation of man from the
beautiful and integrated universe. Man even claims to be equal
to the whole earth. This statement points to the conflicts that
will be the theme of the novel; for if, like other creatures, man
had been integrated fully into his universe, all the conflict
would have been avoided.

Abrahams followed history by making the land the principal cause of the discord between white and black. The South
African earth plays a decisive role in *Wild Conquest*. Its possession is considered the best evidence of one's identity, literally a symbol of being rooted in the earth. In South African
stories and poems the land is always evoked with loving
tenderness, even in works that are primarily urban in tone and
setting. All over southern Africa the rural landscape is the
background of literary sensibility. In *The Path of Thunder*, as
Lanny Swartz returned to the veld and felt happy because the
smell of the earth was in the air, the haunting poetry of Totius
and Pringle slipped through his mind, 'poetry that had captured the soul of the vast undulating expansiveness of the
South African highveld'.[4] South African history has largely
revolved around the problem of land. Throughout *Wild Conquest*, a single theme constantly recurs—the possession of land
as a basis for identity. So, the novel is a true perspective of history. Abrahams does not sentimentalise either the Africans or
the Boers as different writers on each side of the colour line
have done. Rather he views Southern African history more in
terms of what has become known as a 'clash of rival cattle
cultures'.

Of the two conflicting races, the Boers are better portrayed,
both collectively and as individuals. Here Abrahams does not
have to strain after effects, nor does he have to look very far,

70

for all the records are at his disposal. The tone is appropriately Biblical: the Boers consider themselves the children of Israel to be delivered from the British who are the new Egyptians; even their search for a beautiful land where 'a man can live and plant his seed and build his house without anybody standing over him or any flag flying over him',[5] has a Biblical ring which is reinforced by Abrahams' decision to call the section dealing with the Boers, *Bible and Rifle*. These are very simple people, with as much faith in their Bible as in their rifle and the rightness of their cause. Abrahams succeeds in dramatising these qualities in the day-to-day lives of the people. There is the widest range of characters among the Boers, yet Abrahams successfully brings out these differences without tearing the story apart. He uses checks and balances, contrasts and similarities, of the subtlest kind.

First, the Jansen family is presented as a microcosm of the Boer race. On this limited canvas, Abrahams concentrates all attention so that we see what is happening to the whole race. It is only a family of four, including a young boy, but it serves Abrahams' purpose admirably, for there are great differences among its members, and as the story progresses the widening differences between some and the approximation between others becomes fascinating. At the beginning, what greater difference could one get than that between Kasper and his brother, Koos? Slow and deliberate, Kasper is a devoted husband and father. Koos on the other hand is a beast, with all the survival instincts of an animal, underscored by the fact that he gets along well with only animals. Yet after the loss of his valley, Kasper quickly becomes consumed by hatred which begins with the blacks but extends to everything, including his wife and child. At the end it is even probable that he is more animalistic than his brother, for he has had to accomplish a development suddenly which has taken Koos a long period. His earlier deliberateness which had stood his dependants in good stead now makes him a horrible figure as his life becomes dominated by the determination to avenge himself on the blacks.

> They would show these Kaffirs. Good thing about the boy and Koos. Anna was putting the boy against him. Never mind. Koos and the boy were

71

good friends. Koos would see to it that the boy remembered the valley and all that had happened to them. Koos would see to that. Very popular fellow, young Koos. He should go far. Not like that Van As boy. Not at all. A man. Of course, Koos was his brother, his father's son. Blood will tell.

Yes, blood would tell. These days and months had brought him close to his father and the spirit of his people. These days had given him strength. These days, listening and talking to the Commandant and the others, he had felt strength grow in him. They would build a nation founded on strength, just and good. The key to all their future was to know the Kaffirs and deal with them firmly. Meet cunning with cunning, trickery with trickery, watch them all the time... Pity about Anna. Great pity. But she would come to her sense as soon as they were settled. Perhaps before. He had to be firm. A man rules his house and his family. A man is the source of all strength.[6]

Kasper's estrangement from his wife (the equivalent of suppression of personal affections) is underscored by his glorification of his new-found understanding of his race. The herd instinct which draws him towards the other Boers estranges him from his wife who places the highest value on personal relationships. Kasper's election as one of the leaders of the trek, at a time when he is increasingly consumed by hatred and is growing harder inside, points to the changes taking place within the Boers. Kasper, like the other Boers, is clear in his mind about what ought to be done to the blacks; of what he is doing to himself in the process, he does not know, nor does he worry.

Anna is the most successfully portrayed character in the novel. She is a human being in her own right, and at the same time a device, a vehicle for conveying the most important themes of the story. Indeed, the two are interlinked. Her humaneness in spite of the moral wilderness which she and the other Boers go through is an eloquent tribute to the endurance of human nature.

Anna is foremost a foil to her husband. Abrahams' aim is to emphasise that although Kasper's hardness and bitterness may be explained by his having been robbed of his valley it can never amount to a justification. As her husband's identity is linked to the mountain so Anna's is to the valley which had been their home. 'Into this earth had gone a part of her. It had gone very deep. It had spread very wide. The life that was in her was a part of this valley. It was a home.'[7] For Anna, leaving the valley is a traumatic experience, at least as great as her husband's having to forsake his mountain. 'It's like a man walking along the road and suddenly finding that the earth is not beneath his feet and who does not fall but waits for the fall. And goes on waiting.'[8] Yet unlike Kasper and Koos, Anna does not fall into bitterness against the blacks; rather she tries, with pathetic futility, to preserve the future for the Boers; her efforts are frustrated by her husband and Koos who feed her son Stefan with hatred and bitterness.

Abrahams poses Anna's world of private affections against her husband's group identity. The gap between husband and wife widens as Kasper devotes his attention to the trek; and as the trekking party grows each new party seems to drive a wedge between the couple. With time, 'she could feel the physical nature of the wall between them'.[9] Anna, alone on the bank of the Orange River, longs for the private life, laments that her husband no longer sleeps with her, and voices her hatred for the full-tented settlement of the trekkers:

> All the world is turning like Koos. And I, Anna, what am I to do? He thinks of the world of Boers and I think of my world with him and I'm alone. What are we to do whose only wish is to live in peace and with love? Are we wrong?[10]

Ultimately what Anna wants to know is how to cope with the wilderness. And her solution is not to contract our hearts but rather to open them the more; not, as Martinus Van As would have it, to change ourselves to fit our situation, but to expand our hearts to embrace and transform the situation. Who needs, ask the practical Boers, love and affection in time of war? That, Abrahams replies, is needed even more in time of war than at any other time.

To survive, the Boers link themselves together, but Anna counters this herd instinct by achieving a harmony with nature, aided by the baby growing inside her. 'She closed her eyes and thought of the unborn child that was beginning inside her. The empty sadness went from her. The strength of the earth flowed into her.'[11] As the different trekking parties merge and the number of the Boers swells, Anna, who extols humane values above group identity, becomes progressively isolated from her race. Correspondingly, Abrahams intensifies her empathy with the nature around her. When the Van As party reaches the Orange River, it joins the bigger party led by Hendrik Potgieter. Anna, now fully round and even more isolated from her family and her race, retires to the bank of the river and becomes a part of the pregnant and bursting nature around.

> Anna walked along the bank of the river. Low, leaning willows trailed their green tips in the yellowish water. The river was high, swollen with the summer rains; but it was on the way down, for the rains had passed. Underfoot, there was a firmness to the soft earth. The sprouting grass-blades were stiff, full and taught with nourishment. Indeed, the touch of summer plenty was everywhere. The little yellow and gold wild flowers were more erect and scentedly proud than she had ever seen them. And everywhere, intoxicatingly strong, was the scent of the honey that rose from each little flower.
>
> She picked a handful of flowers and raised them to her face. But the overall richness of the honey-kissed air robbed them of their special fragrance. She walked on till she came to a stone on which a big, yellow-bellied frog croaked his last farewell to the late afternoon. Briefly, he turned impudent eyes on her, then carried on, his sides bulging dangerously with his emotional discord. Sundown, earth-smell, a croaking frog, willow trees, and a river. It was good. She sat by the bank of the river, near the croaker, and listened and felt and smelled. She was a little girl in a world of make-believe.[12]

The poetic richness of scenes such as this, which proliferate throughout Book One, right from the invocative opening to Potgieter's exhortation to his people to move on to the promised land, reminds us that Abrahams began his career as a poet, and demonstrates his ability to use symbols effectively.

Anna on the banks of the Orange River sees her world as filled to a bursting ripeness: 'The touch of summer plenty was everywhere.' She notices the contentment of every creature as it is fully integrated into its universe. Anna cannot even enjoy any particular flower because the overall richness of the honey-kissed air robs it of its special fragrance. The frog which turns impudent eyes on her runs the risk of bursting its bulging sides by its single note of emotional discord with the whole scenery. Anna surveys her world and, like the Creator at the beginning of the world, pronounces with satisfaction that 'it is good'. If hers looks like a world of make-believe, it is because at the back of her mind lurks the cruel reality of the Boer world she has sought to escape by journeying to the river bank. Of course, she does not survive the triumph of the new reality. The baby bursts in her just as the battle is joined between the Boers and the Matabele.

'Aaah! It's coming!' the midwife said.

All through the night Anna had screamed. There was a pallor on her face. Her eyes were dark things in deep hollows. There was blood on her mouth, where her lips had been torn by her teeth.

The old woman put one hand into Anna and pressed her stomach with the other in a downward motion. Anna screamed.

'Feel it moving,' the old woman said.

Kasper came near Anna. He put out his hand to touch her head. She pulled away. Hate-filled eyes stared up at him.

'Don't touch me!' There was horror in the cry.

'Delirium,' the old woman said.

'Killer!' Anna cried. It ended on a scream of pain.

'She doesn't know what she's saying,' the old woman said.

'Hate! Devil! Hate!' Anna cried.

'Don't mind it, son,' the old woman said.

'N-o-o-o!' Anna screamed. Her body tossed in agony.

'Go away, Kasper,' Lena said.

Puzzled, hurt, he moved away. She had wanted him near when Stefan was born.

'Now! . . . Water!' the old woman said.

'Killer . . .' The cry died in Anna's throat.

The old woman worked on the bloody mess that was the child!

Lena said: 'Anna . . . Anna . . . Look at Anna!'

'Linen!' the old woman cried.

Lena said: 'She's dead!'

'Water!' the old woman said.

Kasper moved closer and looked at Anna. Her mouth and eyes were open, but she saw nothing and said nothing.

The smack of the old woman's hand resounded loudly. Suddenly, the child cried.

Above the cry of the child was another cry:

'The Kaffirs are coming!' It was everywhere.

'It will live,' the old woman said. She looked at Kasper. 'You have a son.'

He looked at the small thing being wrapped into yards of cloth. He looked at Anna. He looked at Lena. Something in her eyes made him turn away.

From outside, the cry was echoed: 'The Kaffirs are coming! Thousands of them!'

Kasper took his rifle and hurried away.[13]

Anna's final judgment on her husband is more than a personal condemnation; it is the judgment on the whole race, soon to be masters of South Africa, by using the rifle when they could have achieved the same end by using their heads and hearts.

Paul Van As is the conscience of the new day that will dawn with the coming Boer dominance. His recognition, similar to Anna's on the private level, is that the Boers are brutalising themselves in order to master their situation, for in reality they are only losing themselves in order to win. And what a great loss if a nation should lose its soul, even if it gains the whole of southern Africa! Koos' raping of Elsie, Paul's fiancée, the inward-turning of the violence the Boers had used against the blacks, opened Paul's eyes to the dangers the Boers run of being diverted from their ends by the means they are using, that their vision of 'an Afrikaner nation, founded on strength, just and good' is increasingly rendered impossible by the hatred and bitterness that is corroding their humanity. The element of love is missing and, as Paul sees it, for a nation to be just and good it must be founded on love. The Boer emphasis on strength may make for a military triumph over the Matabele, but Paul realises that after victory it will be impossible for hard hearts to turn soft again.

Paul's gentle nature, deeply contrasting with Koos' blood-lust, is presented as an alternative to that of the Boers, for it is not inevitable that the whole race should go the way of the Koos. The hope for a future of peaceful co-existence between the races in South Africa, of an Afrikaner nation, just and good, founded not on strength but on love and humanity, is presented through Paul who has gone to the extent of learning the language of the Baralong, one of the African tribes they have come across on the trek. To the concerted opposition of his people who ostracise him for treating the blacks as if they were white, Paul explains: 'We've got to know them if we are going to live with them.'[14]

Abrahams' ignorance of traditional society seriously weakens his portrayal of the Matabele. The authoritative South African historian De Kiewiet has described the tragedy of the white's failure to see any merit in African society:

At least two generations of settlers grew up in ignorance of the ingenuity and appropriateness with which the natives in their tribal state met the many problems of their lives, in ignorance of the validity of many of the social and moral rules which held them together. European society most easily saw the unattractive aspect of tribal life. It saw the superstition and witchcraft and cruelty. But it failed to see, or saw only imperfectly, the rational structure of tribal life, the protection which it gave the individual, the comfort which it gave his mind, the surveillance which it kept over the distribution of food and land. European society condemned as stagnant and unenlightened a way of life in which happiness and contentment were, for the native, not difficult to find. Between soldier and settler, missionary and magistrate, there was an unvoiced conspiracy against the institutions of the tribe.[15]

Perhaps because he is so thoroughly Westernised, Abrahams' view of the tribal state is much akin to that of the white settlers described above. He begins from the historical fact that the Matabele nation has reached its zenith and started to decline. But there is very little to the lives of the blacks in *Wild Conquest* beyond warfare, superstition and witchcraft. The nation reeks with blood; there is no happiness and contentment here, but fear, mutual suspicion and bloodlust. Abrahams knows nothing about the tribal state—which is perhaps why we are not given any scenes of domestic life: Gubuza's discussions with his wife are about war. In the brief respite he has from his military duties (taken to enable his wife to recuperate from the effects of a gory witchhunt), Dabula goes snake-hunting with his family.

The Matabeles are like people in an historical pageant; they behave exactly as the author wishes, but hardly ever express recognisable thought. Abrahams' imagination even when provided the freest rein does not roam far or wide. The incidents in the Matabele section seem to have been copied from Rider Haggard,[16] as are the people—tempered, of course, by the fact that the writer is an African. Nkomozi, for example, is physically like Gagool, with his bald head, his body shrivelled up like that of a small child, with penetrating eyes which discomfort those he is looking at, and a dry voice, 'dry as when cornstalks are rubbed against each other'.[17] He is not credible as a witch-doctor, and is even less so as the oracle which Abrahams makes him: portrayed as the wise elder in traditional society, Mkomozi lacks modesty; he believes he is the conscience of the nation, freely gives his opinion, and moralises on all issues. That Mkomozi is meant to be our teacher is underlined by his insistence, after delivering each of his homilies, that we should 'remember these words'.

We soon tire of the determination of the Matabele leaders to give 'a few words of wisdom' to their 'children'. There is within the generality of the Matabele people so much throwing out of chests just as there is too much eloquence among their leaders, perhaps because Abrahams feels that oratory is a natural gift of traditional African elders. A reviewer who found pages of *Wild Conquest* 'hard going for the modern reader', probed the author's intentions:

> Mr Abrahams' natives sound like old Vikings, sometimes like the great speechmakers among the American Indians. Again one catches the flavour of what might have been the speech of the Elizabethan explorers. This probably adds a sense of universality and colour to the narrative.[18]

Actually it robs the story of a local habitation and a name, and thus weakens its universal relevance. The characters lose credibility as traditional Africans because too much Western consciousness pervades their awareness.

Ngugi wa Thiong'o, the Kenyan novelist, who praised *Wild Conquest* as an attempt 'to assert the African humanity in face of the Haggardian tradition and naked white racism'[19] has confused intention and achievement. By divorcing them from their surroundings Abrahams robs the Matabele of their humanity. Take, for instance, Abrahams' treatment of witchcraft which, according to Ngugi, shows that traditional African doctors had a knowledge of psychology in the treatment of psychic disorders and disease. E. A. Ritter, in his authoritative *Chaka Zulu* confirmed several oral traditions that Chaka did not believe in witchcraft and was in fact contemptuous of witches. Yet Chaka would not have refuted witchcraft with the distinctly modern psychological arguments we find in Mkomozi's words:

> 'There is no witchcraft except in the mind. Ntongolwane tried to make you believe that you were dying. It was because you accepted the wish of his mind that you could not move or speak. All the time you could move. But your mind told you you could not and you accepted it. Really it was not true. It was

a lie, but your mind accepted the lie and you believed it. That was all . . . Now it is over . . . Now it is over.' As he said them, the words hit him, he wanted to think about them.[20]

Abrahams broadened his theme by contrasting the Matabele and the Boers. The perpetual atmosphere of feasting in Mzilikazi's kingdom fails to conceal omens pointing to the end of Matabele sway. We are repeatedly told: 'Night is over Inzwinyani.' The old age and tiredness of Matabele leaders contrast with the spright confidence of the Boers. The warning is there for the Boers, as Mzilikazi, with the practical mind of Martinus Van As, recounts the growth of the Matabele empire. 'So much blood they had shed on the way. But it was ever so. They had to shed blood, the blood of others, or their own blood would be shed . . . Always bloodletting. To survive, to be free and respected, blood had to flow.'[21] The growing bloodlust among the Boers is meant to be a dramatisation of the bloodlust which had developed among the Matabele as they broke away from Chaka in the east and trekked northwards, a parallel to the Boer trek from the west, also northwards. But the contrast goes deeper, for the bloodlust which the Matabele directed against their neighbours is now directed inwards, culminating in the killing of forty-one innocent people in one night. Perhaps an empire created by the spear will certainly perish when a weapon more potent than the spear appears, but the Matabele empire contains within itself the seeds of its own decay. The wall so elaborately constructed round the capital is meant to secure the kingdom against external foes, but within the palace there are subjects who prove more dangerous to the king because they are very close to him. 'To walk with treachery all day,' Mzilikazi laments, forgetting his own betrayal of Chaka. 'That is painful. It puts a weight on a man's heart.'[22] The king's bloodshot eyes come not only from alcohol but also from insomnia. 'How can a man sleep,' he moans to his favourite wife, 'with blood and treachery around him?'[23] In so far as there is any answer only Mkomozi has it: 'These matters are in the scheme of things.'[24]

Mkomozi's insistence that everything has been preordained

is usually no more than a conviction that the Matabele had pre-determined the nature and life of their empire by the process through which they created it. His long-term vision derives from his role as the link between the past and the present, and between the whites and the blacks. Alone among the Matabele he had seen the whites before, a long time ago, on a trip to the Cape. Now they had come to Matabeleland, and this is also in the scheme of things. 'The matter is out of our hands,' Mkomozi oracularly tells the king and his court. 'This is the change that has to come.'[25]

Abrahams underlines this inevitability by calling the closing section of the book, *A New Day*, making everything as natural as one day succeeding another. He is not saying that the new day ushered in by the Boers will be better than that of the Matabele; it could have been, if the likes of Anna and Paul Van As and the ideals for which they stood had triumphed among the Boers. But it is Koos and his ideas that have gained the upper hand, making it inevitable that the new day would open with fighting and bloodshed. Abrahams forcefully brings out the poignancy of this frustrated hope by making Gubuza and Paul, kindred spirits, kill one another; under different circumstances they would have sat down to learn wisdom from each other. On the point of death, Gubuza and Paul converse and bring out the tragedy in their situation; fear and hatred have become paramount in both camps. The situation appears a little contrived, and could easily degenerate into melodrama, but Abrahams handles it with considerable tact:

> Dying, Gubuza whispered: 'So long since I tilled the earth.'
>
> Paul's eyelids flickered. Elsie nursed his head. He said: 'I, too, have not tilled the earth for many months.'
>
> 'You understand.' Gubuza said. 'Do you all?'
>
> 'No. Only I.'
>
> 'Then you are the one who spoke to my men.'
>
> 'Yes.'
>
> 'Why?'
>
> 'I was for peace.'

'But you killed.'

'There is hate in my people.'

'I am sorry.'

'You are so young ... So young to die. And by my hand.'

'What is your name?'

'Gubuza.'

'You are wise,' Paul said.

But Gubuza did not hear. He had ceased breathing after telling the young man his name.

'What did he say?' Elsie asked.

Paul began to choke.

'Teach ... our ... child.'

Suddenly his body relaxed.[26]

It is significant that on the point of death both Gubuza and Paul lament their divorce from the earth, confirming that alienation between man and his universe which Abrahams sees as the source of all conflicts. As long as one side claims exclusive ownership of the land, discord will never cease. Rather than being the end, the Boers' victory is only the beginning of another tragedy.

The new day dawning in South Africa is significant when we look at the list of those who died that it might be born. True, Koos Jansen is dead, but so are Paul and Gubuza, two of the most humane on both sides. Paul's injunction to his wife to bring up their child in the ways of peace and humanity is stifled by death. Anna, too, is dead. The birth of her baby precisely at the moment that battle was joined signifies that the coming generation will be bloody and harsh. As the last sentence of the novel makes clear the shadow over the land has not lifted: 'Over the land was the shadow of a new day.'[27] As much as the certainty of one day following another, those who have been dispossessed of their land will rise up and fight.

Abrahams' prophecy of a glorious new day for the defeated Matabele is contained in the person of Dabula, captain of Mzilikazi's armies. He is the most interesting character among the Matabele, because he is the only one among them who shows any sign of development. The pattern is familiar in Abrahams, and has been used in the case of Dick Nduli in *Song of the City*, Xuma in *Mine Boy*, and even Lanny Swartz in *The Path of Thunder*: the hero forsakes the narrow background of his village upbringing and develops as he is exposed to new and complex circumstances in the city. Of course, there is no city for Dabula to go to, but he sees the world none the less, on an expedition to recover Mnandi, Mzilikazi's favourite wife, who has been forced to flee the court because of her rival's plottings. The lack of originality technically is underlined by the fact that Abrahams' rationale for sending Dabula on the journey is really to enable us to see life in the court of Moshesh, who is made for this purpose a contemporary of Mzilikazi. Abrahams' construction breaks down completely in this part of the novel and we are able to see in all its crude nakedness the scaffolding of his technique. Instead of the subtle comparisons such as we found in the Boer section, here it is too obvious that characters are introduced merely to act as foils to one another. For instance, the whole point about introducing the Basuto is to provide a foil to the Matabele.

The sum total of Dabula's education is spelt out by Mkomozi. Watching the young warrior in the flawless execution of his duty, the elder statesman had muttered half-approvingly, half-sarcastically: 'So sure for the battle. All the correct orders without thinking . . . So unsure of life.'[28] But the journey to Basutoland broadens Dabula's outlook on life, points him farther on the road towards the wisdom achieved by Gubuza, his foster-father, who also had visited Moshesh. The Basuto king's rebuke of Dabula is meant for the whole of the Matabele: 'When a man has lived by the spear, it is difficult, sometimes impossible, for him to learn to live by his head.'[29] This is the morality which Abrahams wants the blacks to carry into the future, and it is one lesson that Dabula does not miss. With his mission successfully accomplished, Mkomozi congratulates him, 'Now life is real for you, my son. It will never again be just a spear and a battle cry.'[30] Dabula, as the custodian of Lobengula, the heir-apparent of the future empire across the Limpopo, is made the new conscience of his race. Thus, at the end of the novel, as the Matabele evacuate their capital to make a new beginning elsewhere, and while Mzilikazi mourns over his loss, Dabula firmly sets his face northwards, leading his own son with one hand and Lobengula with the other towards a new land and a new destiny.

NOTES

[1] *Wild Conquest* (Faber and Faber, London, 1951). All references are to this edition.
[2] *Ibid.*, p. 52.
[3] *Ibid.*, pp. 13–14.
[4] *The Path of Thunder*, p. 17.
[5] *Wild Conquest*, p. 93.
[6] *Ibid.*, p. 340.
[7] *Ibid.*, p. 59.
[8] *Ibid.*, p. 59.
[9] *Ibid.*, p. 80.
[10] *Ibid.*, p. 135.
[11] *Ibid.*, p. 84.
[12] *Ibid.*, p. 148.
[13] *Ibid.*, pp. 369–70.
[14] *Ibid.*, p. 297.
[15] C. W. De Kiewiet, *A History of South Africa* (Oxford University Press, London, 1957), p. 86.
[16] Actually Abrahams had relied upon, almost to the point of plagiarism, Solomon Plaatje's *Mhudi* (1930), the first novel in English by a South African non-white. The mission-trained Plaatje's portrayal of traditional society was Haggardian.
[17] *Wild Conquest*, p. 189.
[18] Christine Govan in *Saturday Review of Literature*, 33 (June 17, 1950), p. 21.
[19] Ngugi wa Thiong'o, *Homecoming* (Heinemann, London, 1972), p. 43.
[20] *Wild Conquest*, p. 261.
[21] *Ibid.*, p. 182.
[22] *Ibid.*, p. 257.
[23] *Ibid.*, p. 187.
[24] *Ibid.*, p. 258.
[25] *Ibid.*, p. 351.
[26] *Ibid.*, pp. 379–80.
[27] *Ibid.*, p. 383.
[28] *Ibid.*, p. 218.
[29] *Ibid.*, p. 306.
[30] *Ibid.*, p. 365.

Chapter Six
Tell Freedom

In her Ann Radcliffe Memorial lecture at Harvard in 1961, the South African novelist, Nadine Gordimer, speaking on *The Novel and the Nation in South Africa*, lamented that with the exception of Abrahams' there were no other English novels written by black South Africans for her to discuss. True, there were short stories and essays, but black South African writers have mostly produced autobiographies, partly because they feared the different and greater demands made by the novel, but mainly because they were so anxious to take advantage of the easy opportunity to use their talents to satisfy the curiosity of their own nation and other nations who were interested in the country's problems. 'This sort of writing,' Miss Gordimer pronounced, 'however interesting, may make a competent journalist, but does not make a creative writer. And if a man has it in him to create, he should not squander the stuff of his experience.'[1] Yet it is noteworthy that it was both the autobiographical *Return to Goli* and, more particularly, *Tell Freedom*[2] that won Abrahams international acclaim. The wide attention given to these two books and the relative neglect of Abrahams' novels shows that readers were more interested in satisfying their 'curiosity' about conditions in South Africa than in literary merits. The well-known anthropologist, M. J. Herskovits, spoke for many when he reviewed *Tell Freedom*:

> . . . a beautifully written, moving, revealing story. It adds an essential dimension to the African picture, for the African of colour, either in the Union of South Africa or in the rest of the continent, rarely speaks with such forthrightness and literary talent. Aside from the emotional experience books of this kind can yield, their first-hand testimony about the underside of the interracial situation gives them great sociological importance.[3]

Tell Freedom has received more attention for its 'sociological importance' but it possesses considerable literary merit. In spite of its episodic nature it is a very organised book, the unifying theme being how Abrahams successfully escaped from conditions which have crippled his family, friends, acquaintances from childhood and most others from his race. So, a persistent Crusoeism pervades the book; every incident points out the author's yearning to break away from his surroundings and achieve his dream outside his country. The book opens on this note:

> I pushed my nose and lips against the pane and tried to lick a raindrop sliding down on the other side. As it slid past my eyes, I saw the many colours in the raindrop ... It must be warm in there. Warm and dry. And perhaps the sun would be shining in there. The green must be the trees and the grass; and the brightness, the sun ... I was inside the raindrop, away from the misery of the cold damp room. I was in a place of warmth and sunshine, inside my raindrop world.
> 'Lee.'
> The sound jerked me out of my raindrop world. I was at the window, looking out, feeling damp.
> 'Lee.'
> I sensed that that was the sound by which I was identified.[4]

The main theme of *Tell Freedom* is a search for a place in the sun; it is this quest that gives direction to Abrahams' life. Two worlds are presented to us above: the encapsuled world made by the raindrop, 'a place of warmth and sunshine', where he wants to be, in contrast to the abject reality in which he is forced to dwell. In the rest of the book this polarity is widened to embrace South Africa as a whole where Abrahams does not want to be, and the outside world, a place of freedom into which he wants to escape. South Africa is not the place for a black boy to dream, and the voice which jerks him back to reality—his father's voice—is recalled at the end when Abrahams walks away from South Africa and, in his own words, 'all my dreams walked with me'.[5]

86

Loss is an inevitable theme in any autobiography, but it takes a particularly poignant tone in autobiographies by blacks. In South Africa it takes the form of continuous deprivation. Abrahams attempts to make order out of the instability that is the lot of all non-whites in South Africa by always providing an avenue for escape from the stultifying situation. For example, the death of his father introduces the young Abrahams to a bigger world, his first visit to town, at Fordsburg where he has to take a train. Yet, Elsburg his destination is in fact a dead end, and Abrahams emphasises this by describing his daily routine before describing his foster-parents, Aunt Liza and her husband Uncle Sam, and indeed his first day at Elsburg. When finally he talks about his first day in the location, it is to point out that it is not the place for him:

> The place, itself, seemed to fit into the bleak austerity of the land about it. There was not a tree in the valley below. To the east and west there was just the harshness of the sloping land under the curving sky. Even the sky seemed cold and remote and very far away.
>
> Only the river promised a touch of softness in this hard place. A line of willows marked the course it took. They were the only trees in all the land about. I would go there, I promised myself. I would go down to the river and look at the trees.
>
> Aunt Liza came out of the house. My five minutes were up. She gave me two pails.
>
> 'The well is up the street.'
>
> I took the pails and marched out of the gate.[6]

It is difficult to miss the similarity between this passage and the opening of the book, which in fact it seems to duplicate: the cruel reality of the here and now, from which the youth tries to escape by inventing his own world (from the material at hand), only to be rudely jerked back to reality, by the voices of his parent or parent-surrogate.

And the reality of his life, at such an impressionable age, in Elsburg is frightening. A typical passage has to be quoted in spite of its considerable length. On his first day in Elsburg, Abrahams joins the other boys in looking for cow dungs

87

which their parents use for cooking and heating the pressing irons.

We darted here and there, grabbing the dried flat cakes and shoving them into our sacks. We were not children at play. This was serious. Life depended on this. To the left of me, two boys argued over a piece of dung both had spotted at the same time. They soon came to blows. The rest were too concerned with finding dung to stop and look. I lost my nervousness of the cows and darted among them, grabbing pieces of dung. I saw a huge piece and dashed for it. Another boy had seen it at the same time. We glared at each other. Two savage dogs over a bone. I remember I was the stranger. I had to install myself before I could expect to fight on terms of equality. I veered away and left the precious piece to him.

I filled one sack and started on the next. But now the dung became more rare. Competition became fiercer. There were more dog-fights. I passed a boy on his knees, blood dripping from his nose. Two little girls were pulling each other's hair. I bumped into a boy. He pushed me over. I jumped up. He waited, his fists bunched, ready for the fight. I looked into his eyes and it seemed he was as frightened as I was. Somehow, seeing fear in his eyes made me fell less of an outsider. I turned my back on him. I heaved the full sack on to my back and trotted away scanning the grass. I was beginning to recognise the cakes at quite a distance. The boy cursed me, a frustrated desperation in his voice.

All about me, each with sacks on his or her back, children ran; they darted first this way, then that: they stooped, grabbed, shoved dung into their sacks and were off again. The area of search widened till we ceased to be a group, till we lost contact with each other.

When I had filled both my sacks the sun was high and I was alone in a hollow strip of land. I flopped down on the ground and leaned against the sacks. I

was utterly wearied. It was not just tiredness. There
had been a tight desperation in the search, a nervous
tension. Now it was over I felt listless.

After a while I got up. I now had to find my way
home. There was not a person in sight. If I faced
about the river would be on my right, and if I veered
slightly to the left, I would be going in the general
direction of home.

I heaved the sacks on to my back and climbed out
of the hollow strip. I walked steadily, anxiously, yet
wearily, till I topped a slight rising. The cows grazed
in the valley below. I was right. That was the way
home. And down there, among the cows, were
some of the children. To the left, some way behind
me, were others. Yet others were far ahead, on their
way home. I trudged down into the valley. I met up
with some of the children and we walked in silence,
each bent under the weight of dung.[7]

Hogarth could not have painted a more memorable canvas.
Abrahams' success above depends on the use of short sentences to build up an atmosphere of tension—the usual recipe
in his early fiction. The success of such passages as that above
has not gone unnoticed, inviting comparison with Abrahams'
fictional writing, usually leading to a denigration of the
novels. Actually he was capable right from the beginning of
writing such material. The only difference is their place in an
autobiography vis-à-vis a work of fiction. The above, it
should be noted, is a complete episode in itself. Abrahams
never fails in his novels to pull off such incidents. However, a
novel needs to be more than a string of episodes, however
tense. In an autobiography there is no need to invest the book
with any conscious unity; the mere fact that all incidents are
filtered through the author's consciousness is enough. In his
novels Abrahams never fails in dramatising specific incidents;
where he fails is in making these incidents fuse into a powerful
whole.

Not only his strengths, but Abrahams' weaknesses, are
found in *Tell Freedom*, and if they do not attract that much
attention it is because the demands of a novel and those of an

autobiography are totally different. Take, for instance, characterisation, on which Abrahams has always scored poorly. The characters in *Tell Freedom* are as wooden as in any of his novels. As we become engrossed in the opening pages we may forget that there is very little of his parents there, in spite of the long discourse on his father's genealogical tree; we may forget that there is nothing to remember Aunt Liza except by her thick biceps, as she washes during daytime, and irons at night; or that her husband, Uncle Sam, who goes to work before dawn and returns at dusk, is a fleeting presence, long and thin. It is when we get back to Vrededorp that Abrahams makes a determined attempt at presenting his characters, and the result is very interesting, especially when we consider their closeness to the people in *Mine Boy*, for here is the setting of that novel. Indeed, an inventory of the real life characters in *Tell Freedom* is like a run-down of the characters in *Mine Boy*.

The two characters described at some detail in *Tell Freedom* belong to Abrahams' Vrededorp years. The similarities between Granny Petersen, Mkomozi of *Wild Conquest*, and Aunt Tante of *The Path of Thunder* are very remarkable. The conclusion must be that Abrahams has certain figures indelibly fixed in his mind which he uses as prototypes, Granny Petersen being in this case the archetype of the old (and wise) man or woman, as the opportunity demands. This point is buttressed by Abrahams' long description of Oupa Ruiter, concluding: 'He was a symbol of something important to all the citizens of Vrededorp.'[8] People to Abrahams, whether fictional or real-life, are always more important as symbols than just human beings. The distance in time between the writing of his autobiography and his youth when Abrahams knew Oupa Ruiter and Granny Petersen is compensated for by the historicity he gives, for example, to the non-white characters in *Wild Conquest*. But it would be correct to say that Abrahams did not really know these people; his knowledge of them stems from his youth. It has the same impact on us as reading about black figures in history books. Their forms had been fixed in his mind, but how to translate them into living characters beyond the narrow confines, and the brief period, in which he knew them, became a problem in his novels.

What saves Abrahams in *Tell Freedom* is that there is no need to develop these characters; each makes his brief appearance and bows out. What links them together is that they and the author interact briefly, before each goes his own way. Or rather, unlike Abrahams, these characters have nowhere to go: they are trapped in Vrededorp. The question is how Abrahams is going to escape, or become spiritually atrophied like them. Very early in *Tell Freedom* escapism becomes an overt theme, and Abrahams' yearning often breaks out dramatically. On a visit to his mother he separates himself from his family, runs to the top of a hill and, feeling over-powered by a strong sense of grandeur, shouts at the top of his voice for Nondi whose voice seems to come back to him a long, long way off. 'I opened my arms wide. And it was as if I embraced all the land I looked upon, and all the people who lived in the land. An irrepressible shout swelled up in me and I let it out with all the power of my lungs. "Y-a-h-o-o!"'[9] At another time, when he visits his brother Harry, now in jail, whom he finds with a gang of fellow prisoners breaking stones, Abrahams is smitten by the sight of an eagle flying overhead: 'I longed, suddenly, to be like that eagle, able to fly right out of the range of this place, so that I would not have to watch my brother breaking rock under the hot sun.'[10] In spite of their theatricality all these episodes add up to a powerful picture of a soul desperately yearning to fly, for everything around him reminds him of his social claustrophobia.

However, even if we can be sure that the incidents happened exactly as Abrahams has recorded them—it requires an extraordinary feat of memory to recall details of conversations at such a distance in time—we soon become suspicious that this is the adult Abrahams looking back on the incidents and recognising with hindsight what important landmarks they were in his life. Too often, casual words would later assume the importance which they could not have had at that time. *Tell Freedom* is overtly selective: an incident is selected because it has contributed to the making of the artist, and is recorded in such a fashion as to invest the most mundane words and occasions with the most far-reaching import. Indeed, this is the only link between all the vignettes showing the young Abrahams in school—down to such details as his inevitable proficiency in English, and deficiency in Arithmetic: the hand of destiny is read into these things. His remembrance of his school days closes with his school mistress reading the Everyman text to him: 'Everyman, I will go with thee and be thy guide in thy most need to go by thy side.' And Abrahams promises to find the deep meaning of these words one day. The mistress dismisses him: 'Run along, Peter.'[11] A casual remark, almost a school slang, but Abrahams builds it into something of moment; and he sprints along the road of destiny—with a little help from his friends.

Awareness, coming with age and education, merely alienates the black youth further from the reality that it reveals to him with increasing clarity. Abrahams' problem is to reconcile the dream-world opened to him by his education with the abject reality allowed him by his monolithic society. But that element of luck which he hammers upon whenever he compares his lot with that of his friends and relatives invariably comes to his aid, and soon becomes a major motif in *Tell Freedom*. He takes us through incidents all of which show the worsening of the conditions of his brothers, sisters, and friends; but Abrahams is either an indifferent observer of most of these things, or his longing to escape has become so obsessive that it makes him, however unconsciously, subtract himself at all times from all that is going on around him.

> I was ripe for something new, the new things my books had revealed, to take the place of the old life. But what? And how was I to achieve it? I felt lonely and longed for something without being able to give it a name. The horizons of Vrededorp were inadequate. Where was I to find the new horizons of my needs?[12]

Luck leads him to the Bantu Social Club: 'But for the huge sign on its front, I would have passed it by as just another European building.'[13] Inside, he joins the company of assertive soul brothers, W. E. B. Du Bois, J. Weldon Johnson, and other black American writers, as a result of which he feels his outlook on life transformed, and he becomes 'a colour nationalist through the writings of men and women who lived a world away from me. To them I owe a great debt for crystallizing my vague yearning to write and for showing me the long dream was attainable.'[14] Yet because of his earlier exposure to English romantic poets and their preoccupation with freedom, Abrahams opts to go to England.

> Perhaps I would go to America afterwards. But I would go to England first. I would go there because the dead men who called were, for me, more alive than the most vitally living. In my heart I knew my going there would be in the nature of a pilgrimage.[15]

The rest of the story is taken up with how this dream is realised. Also, from this point *Tell Freedom* becomes less interesting, as Abrahams becomes bogged down in figures of how he spends a wage of a pound a week, and dates and events. He joins the Coloured wing of the Boy Scout movement, the Pathfinders—the name seems to have a personal symbolic importance for him, so tailored is the whole story to his finding his way out of South Africa—and enrols in a correspondence course. Henceforth, the consciousness of the adult Abrahams intrudes palpably on the incidents. Even when he is admitted to the Diocesan Training College, Grace Dieu, near Pietersburg, in spite of the sorrow of the whole family, his mother's consolation is that he has at last found a way out of the rut that is Vrededorp: 'As we walked away from Vrededorp, my mother said heavily: "It is a bad place. I'm glad you are going out of it."'[16] Inevitably, the poverty of the world he is leaving behind conditions Abrahams' response to the College, which he feels has lived up to the name of the Grace of God. The tenor of writing here, especially Abrahams' fulsome praise for his white teachers represents something of a spiritual achievement, especially when we remember that two years earlier he had just finished *Return to Goli* where he condemned virtually all whites in particularly scathing terms. One of the short stories in *Dark Testament*, *From an Unfinished Novel*, owes its origin to Abrahams' experience at Grace Dieu, and that story shows well enough that racialism lurks under the surface.

Abrahams' experience at Grace Dieu has deeply influenced his art. In the whole college, he has four friends, and, by his own admission, two of them pull with him because they share a common city background. His detachment from his 'special

93

' friends'—even if we grant that this is emotion recollected in tranquillity—is remarkable for its lack of passion, and borders on thinly disguised contempt in the case of the colour nationalists who identify so closely with Joe Louis, the black American boxer. Abrahams' aloofness is not lost on his family when he goes home on holidays; his withdrawn manners contrast with their vivacity, and his sister calls his attention to it. Abrahams admits: 'Because she made me aware of it, I realise I had changed. I had a new, seeing coldness that had nothing to do with coldness of feeling.'[17] In spite of the slightly defensive posture, Abrahams surely feels there is nothing to be ashamed of in his new attitude, and in fact seems to approve of it as the product of superior intelligence—'a new, seeing coldness'—which has little to do with emotions. That he feels this is an inevitable preserve of the educated is evidenced in his novels where the educated Africans are shown as superior to and aloof from their people. His return to his birth-place, his family, or his friends, the unfortunate members of the gang whom he had left behind, fails to move him emotionally. Abrahams never succeeds in drumming up warmth for the common people, or in portraying them successfully.

St Peter's College, where Abrahams goes after quitting Grace Dieu has even a more decisive influence on his life and art. As at the former college the teachers live up to expectation. But of more importance is a young Jewish couple:

> the first white people to invite me to their home as a guest, the first white people who had sat at a table with me. Gradually, over a period of time, they had nursed my friendship, had made me see that it was something they valued and desired. Then, in easy stages, they had offered an explanation of all the things that had obsessed me: colour and the error Jonathan and I had found in the religious equation.[18]

This is the couple which figured in the short story, *Jewish Sister* of *Dark Testament*. In fact, the prominence of Jews in Abrahams' earlier books and the very favourable light in which they were invariably portrayed must have derived from the influence of this couple. As he explained in *Jewish Sister*, Abrahams does not find spiritual satisfaction at St

Peter's, and this probably explains his attachment to the Jewish couple, with whom he spends 'many nights and afternoons of reading and discussion. Things to be learnt, problems to be worked out. And understanding seemed to be just round the corner. And there was something bigger than hate to live for ...'[19] How well the lessons are learnt we can see by noting the woman's gentle admonishment in the short story which has formed the substance of Abrahams' message for the greater part of his writing career:

> '... What do you get out of hating people, out of having this bitterness in your heart always? It doesn't make you happy. Things are wrong. Terribly wrong. But what can you do about it if you only hate? Supposing all your poems were to be poems of hate, would they serve any purpose? But supposing you were to describe the suffering not only of yourself but of your people, and suggested some ways to change condition, would that not be much more useful? So far you have just been thinking of yourself and your own suffering. Your own pride has been hurt. You know that you are the equal of the white man, and he denies you the chance to prove it. But there are others, who feel the same way. You have an advantage over them, you have education. Why not use it to show them that hate won't get you anywhere, but that calmly, and with clear minds, they must work to remedy wrongs?[20]

As always for Abrahams, personal and artistic creeds go hand in hand, and he believes the experience with the Jewish couple has made him both a better man and a better writer. The couple introduce him to Marxism, which he undoubtedly accepts completely in the first flush of friendship, although he seems anxious to prove in *Tell Freedom* that the rift is there right from the beginning. True, his communist characters fail by the test of humaneness—which is Abrahams' only valid yardstick in his earlier years—however praiseworthy their earnestness, but this probably reflects the experience of the communists under whom he worked in London.[21] The uncritical acceptance and doctrinaire stance of some of the stories in *Dark Testament* and 'the Marxian theories of economics and imperialism' by which he sought to explain the racialism of South Africa in *Mine Boy*, better represent Abrahams' attitude towards Marxism in the earlier years.

Abrahams devotes the rest of *Tell Freedom* to how he has to keep moving, literally running, in order to avoid becoming embroiled in the factional hatred within the Marxist movement, which he sometimes seems to dread more than the racialism of the land. 'I wanted to believe in the New Future that promised equality and security of all men. If only they had room for pity, compassion, and mercy . . .If only they allowed for the human heart . . .'[22] First from Johannesburg to Cape Town, and from an affluent suburb of the latter to District Six, the poor Coloured location (the hero of *The Path of Thunder* had lived here), Abrahams finally arrived in Durban on a scorching day in June 1939, and became a guest of the Indian nationalist movement, the Liberal Study Group, which 'welcomed me as one of their own'.[23] Characters known at this period later find their way into his fiction, in *A Night of Their Own*.

Inevitably, Abrahams got into trouble with the police who suspected him of being a communist—which he denied. When the Second World War broke out, the country went into a crisis (this provided material later used in *Song of the City*) and he signed on a ship in need of a whole crew. Because of his communist sympathies, the police were willing—almost eager—to let him go. So, finally he was free, unwanted to the last. The night before his departure he consciously underwent a symbolic act of cleansing, by swimming in the ocean.

> With my eyes on the stars, I took stock and searched for the meaning of life in terms of the life I had known in this land for nearly twenty-one years.
> All my life had been dominated by a sign, often invisible but no less real for that, which said:
> RESERVED FOR EUROPEANS ONLY
> Because of that sign I had been born into the filth and squalor of the slums and had spent nearly all my childhood and youth there; because of it a whole

generation, many generations, had been born, had grown up and died amid the filth and squalor of the slums. I had the marks of rickets on my body; but I was only one of many, not unique. I had had to go to work before I went to school. Many had never gone to school. Free compulsory education was 'Reserved for Europeans only'. All that was finest and best in life was 'Reserved for Europeans only'. The world, today, belonged to the 'Europeans'.

And in my contacts with them, the Europeans had made it clear that they were the overlords, that the earth and all its wealth belonged to them. They had spoken the language of physical strength, the language of force. And I had submitted to their superior strength. But submission can be a subtle thing. A man can submit today in order to resist tomorrow. My submission had been such. And because I had not been free to show my real feeling, to voice my true thoughts, my submission had bred bitterness and anger. And there were nearly ten million others who had submitted with equal anger and bitterness. One day, the whites would have to reckon with these people. One day their sons and daughters would have to face the wrath of these embittered people. The two million whites cannot for ever be overlords of the ten million non-whites. One day they may have to submit to the same judgement of force they have invoked in their dealings with us . . .

For me, personally, life in South Africa had come to an end. I had been lucky in some of the whites I had met. Meeting them had made a straight 'all-blacks-are-good-all-whites-are-bad' attitude impossible. But I had reached a point where the gestures of even my friends among the whites were suspect, so I had to go or be for ever lost. I needed, not friends, not gestures, but my manhood. And the need was desperate.

Perhaps life had a meaning that transcended race and colour. If it had, I could not find it in South Africa. Also, there was the need to write, to tell freedom, and for this I needed to be personally frcc . . .

When the first rays of the morning sun touched the sky in the east I got up and dressed. The long night was over. This was the moment of departure. I felt in my pocket. The three pounds were still there.

I walked briskly down to the docks. And all my dreams walked with me.[24]

We can see why Abrahams felt little ambivalence towards leaving South Africa: his dream could never be fulfilled there. His book ends on an assured note, a sharp contrast to the anguish of Ezekiel Mphahlele in *Down Second Avenue* (1959), Bloke Modisane in *Blame Me on History* (1963), Alfred Hutchinson in *Road to Ghana* (1965), and less successful autobiographies by black South Africans. We can also see why the dawn has assumed such a symbolic significance in Abrahams' novels. He left with the first rays of the morning sun. 'The long night was over.' Abrahams has remained convinced that the night will end for his people too, and that they will one day find a place in the sun. The hint of embittered anger on the last two pages is the only dark cloud in a story that is remarkably free of bitterness. The conditions against which the young Abrahams struggled would lead us to expect a warped nature, seared through by bitterness. But both the man and his story are saved by his profound compassion.

NOTES

[1] *The Times Literary Supplement*, August 11, 1961, p. 522.
[2] *Tell Freedom* (Faber and Faber, London, 1954). All page references are to this edition.
[3] *Nation*, 179 (August 21, 1954), p. 154.
[4] *Tell Freedom*, p. 9.
[5] *Ibid.*, p. 311.
[6] *Ibid.*, p. 19.
[7] *Ibid.*, pp. 25–6.
[8] *Ibid.*, p. 74.
[9] *Ibid.*, p. 124.
[10] *Ibid.*, p. 136.
[11] *Ibid.*, p. 160.
[12] *Ibid.*, p. 163.
[13] *Ibid.*, p. 190.
[14] *Ibid.*, p. 197.
[15] *Ibid.*, p. 200.
[16] *Ibid.*, p. 217.
[17] *Ibid.*, p. 228.
[18] *Ibid.*, p. 250.
[19] *Dark Testament*, pp. 32–3.
[20] *Ibid.*, p. 32.
[21] *Return to Goli*, p. 16.
[22] *Tell Freedom*, p. 274.
[23] *Ibid.*, p. 304.
[24] *Ibid.*, pp. 310–11.

Chapter Seven

A Wreath for Udomo

A Wreath for Udomo[1] begins the political phase in Abrahams' writing career. Unfortunately, but perhaps not unexpectedly, his subsequent novels have received more attention for their political postures than their literary qualities. In Africa generally, but especially in Ghana, *A Wreath* was greeted with a stormy protest, because the setting was too close, and the prophecy too foreboding, for the young nations then on the threshold of independence [Colonial Gold Coast became independent Ghana the year after the novel was published]. The whole thrust of the novel was found unpalatable—particularly that a truly dedicated African leader could betray African freedom fighters (most of whom were congregating in Ghana even so early) to white racists—all in the interest of his own nation, or all of Africa, however defined! Very little attention has been paid to the fact that this is a novel, not a political tract, deserving consideration as a work of art. Had its critics examined the novel with the detachment with which Abrahams himself viewed the African political scene, they would have been able to make a more relevant and more lasting judgment.

The main strength of *A Wreath*, as we have come to expect from Abrahams, derives from the portrayal of people and incidents he knows very well. In fact, the first section of the book, entitled *The Dream*, and centred in London, is what really holds the novel up. The group of African exiles in London, calling themselves, in the words of Tom Lanwood their self-appointed leader, 'a sort of brains trust behind the anti-colonial organisations in this country', are rootless people living a bohemian kind of life. Collectively, their lives are summed up by the word 'dream', and it is a dream which is very much divorced from the African reality (most of them are from Panafrica, but do not know what is happening in

99

Pluralia). Paul Mabi, although one of them, sums them up with the detachment of an artist:

> Of our own free will, if there is such a thing, we've elected to live for a cause. We would liberate a continent. That is what we live for. Someone once told me we are the lost generation: we don't belong to the past of our own people and we have not found a place in your world ...[2]

Abrahams knows this group very well, for he is indeed one of them, in spite of his criticism of their preoccupation with politics. Their attachment to Africa, and the overtly sentimental tone in which this attachment is couched, is something that the exiled Abrahams himself understands and shares. 'Africa!' the usually taciturn Udomo apostrophises on one occasion. 'She is a little like a heart. Africa is my heart, the heart of all of us who are black. Without her we are nothing: while she is not free we are not men. That is why we must free her, or die. That is how it is.'[3] Simply by staying away from home the exile risks being accused of betrayal to the true interests of the mass of his people and of being ignorant of what is happening at home, as Udomo and the others are repeatedly accused during the Progress Party lecture. Always he has to debate within himself—as we see with Mhendi, who has run away from persecution—whether he has not allowed commitment to the self to override to the struggle. His reply invariably takes the form of an affirmation, to Africa as a spiritual home rather than a geographical reality, to the whole continent as a concept rather than any particular part of it. On his last day at sea, Udomo looks towards land in the darkness of night, and although he cannot see, he feels Africa 'out there', and invokes its aid for his life mission:

> Mother Africa! Oh, Mother Africa, make me strong for the work I must do. Don't forget me in the many you nurse. I would make you great. I would have the world respect you and your children. I would have the sun of freedom shine over you once more. It was for this I left you for so long and lived in strange lands among strange people and

suffered and was abused and was cold and hungry. It was in order to come back to free you, to free all your children, and to make you great among those who now look down on you. They do not understand your dark ways. For them you are something to be exploited, and your children creatures to be held down. Now this must end. I will end it if you help me. I cannot see you but I can feel you out there in the dark. Tomorrow I will be with you, in you. Do not let me get lost in your many. Help me, watch me, guide me. My name is Michael Udomo. Do not forget it; Michael Udomo, the instrument of your freedom ...[4]

Individually, the characters are not so successfully portrayed. Adebhoy flits in and out of the group, both in London and back home in Panafrica, but his personality is lost in his portrayal as the backsliding revolutionary, who goes back to tribalism and the past (the two terms are synonymous in this novel) in spite of his training as a doctor. He sanctions voodoo killing, drinks and eats too much, and has grown too fat. Tom Lanwood (modelled after the late George Padmore, Nkrumah's West Indian political adviser), is the self-appointed apologist of the African revolution who is betrayed by the realities of Africa, and returns 'home' (as he calls London) to die, frustrated, disillusioned and embittered. Mhendi, too, in spite of Abrahams' approval of his unflagging dedication, belongs here. He is a true Abrahams hero, for like Lanny Swartz in *The Path of Thunder*, his generosity of soul even extends to the racists who had killed thousands of his people, including his wife, and seized their land. To his new consort who opines that the white rulers of Pluralia are born evil, Mhendi replies firmly: 'They are not born evil. They are human, as you and I. As with us, some of them are kind and others are cruel. The things they do, they do out of a fear that has grown so great that it has become a thing of evil ...'[5] This openness of mind makes him the only true kindred spirit of Udomo who, with unwonted candour, regrets that Mhendi was not born in Panafrica—and then proceeds to betray him to his enemies. It is Mhendi who finally wins because, perhaps more than any other character, he influences our final opinion of Udomo.

The key incident is that last meeting between the two, when Udomo skilfully obtains the information about Mhendi's jungle hideout which the white racists need. Admittedly, with the best will it is something difficult to pull off, the betrayal of a friend for whatever reason. But Abrahams in attempting to load the dice in favour of Udomo actually works against him. Mhendi's warm and relaxed mood contrasts with Udomo's tenseness and secrecy, although Abrahams attributes the latter quality to the burden of office, not just something put on for the occasion. The whole cat-and-mouse nature of the encounter, with Udomo's reminder about the wrong judgment by generations unborn to show that he is at least constantly aware of the momentous occasion, and finally Mhendi's unwitting signing of his own death warrant in his admission that he would probably have done the same thing under similar circumstances: all this is meant to soften our feelings towards Udomo, if not exonerate him altogether, but it still leaves a nasty taste in the mouth.

When at last he is caught, Mhendi's mind goes back to this interview. Here are his last thoughts before his captors murder him:

> Really, Udomo told me why he was selling me. Told me clearly and I couldn't see it. Asked me, and I told him what to do. Terribly literal person. I couldn't do this, no matter what I said to him. Or could I? How can I know until I'm faced with it, as he was faced ... Soon, now. Very soon now. How does one pray? Does one say: God, I have done my duty, I have tried to help liberate my people, and for that I must die? Is that a prayer? What is prayer? Maria. God, *please*, please take care of Maria. Her only crime was to love me; mine, to keep her with me. Take care of her, *please*.[6]

In spite of this last display of his usual generosity of mind Mhendi of course does not succeed in lightening his friend's guilt, although this must have been Abrahams' intention. Indeed, Mhendi makes it worse. His prayer begins with his public duty and ends on a personal note, hitting on the conflict between public and private moralities which is at the heart of the novel. It is Mhendi who really wins by giving his last thoughts to his mistress, a clear repudiation of Udomo's betrayal of Lois in London, and his betrayal of Mhendi himself in Africa. Abrahams seems to be confused here. Udomo's copious tears—Abrahams' usual device to elicit our sympathy—do not change the fact that Udomo has failed again by the yardstick set by the author himself. To Paul Mabi he pleads extenuating circumstances, but the latter confesses his inability to understand the Prime Minister's position. 'I can only see the selling of a friend!' snaps Mabi, and quits the Cabinet and the country in a hurry.

Paul Mabi, the 'authorial' character, is not a new figure in Abrahams' gallery of characters—his physical description is practically a carbon-copy of Mako's—although this is the first time Abrahams has linked his hero with the visual arts. The process will be repeated in the next book, *A Night of Their Own*, where once again Nkosi's physical description is exactly that of Mabi and Mako, leading one to suspect that Abrahams might have had a real-life model in mind. We may dispute whether an artistic vocation confers on a character any special ability as an analyst of human behaviour, but Abrahams' notion is that his artists are able to see through the façade and get to the essence of human character and motivation. Mabi's deep sense of history, combined with a deep moral awareness, qualifies him as the author's mask—practically all the lamentations about the evils of tribalism come from Paul Mabi—and gives him the insight to recognise and state the central conflict of the novel, which he does with a fitting awareness of history, on the first night of his return to Africa, recalled to cap Udomo's political achievement by delivering the votes of his people to the ruling party. He looks backwards and forwards, in reminiscences addressed to Lois:

> Mabi went to the window. Could one see this orchestra of creatures? As a boy he fancied he had seen them. But he knew it was only a fancy grown to the point of reality by the passage of time. And tomorrow he would be home among his own

people. He dreaded it a little. They would be the same and he would be changed. Fortunate that the mountain people were less demonstrative than the people of the plains. It would be good to see his old mother again. But first there'd be that awful ritual before he could take her in his arms. Still ...

And Lois ∴. What was the piece of claptrap with which he'd justified this betrayal of her? Adebhoy had used it: *The cause is greater than personalities.* A good umbrella under which to betray one's friends, and the damnable thing is that one did it ... Oh, Lois ... Forgive me. There is something compelling in this African cry for light that I cannot resist. Perhaps it is because they don't even know they cry for light. Is that justification for betraying one's friend? Can the betrayal of the lowliest friend ever be justified? To you it's always been clear; and to me, for moments, too. But what of this Africa that shaped me? Which is the choice: to betray you or to betray the dream? Is the choice always between two evils? Never between good and evil? If it is, then it is the cruellest for us. It is always the generation in transition that has to make the cruellest choice of all.[7]

Mabi's reading of history—that the first generation of African leaders are trapped men, betrayed by circumstances, and made morally culpable by the options open to them—will be disputed by many, for it comes close to self-justification. This is Udomo's plea, but Mabi does not find it difficult to make up his mind at the critical time. The Mabi who stomps out of the country is a credible, even noble, creature, for the choice has always been clear to him. Unfortunately if he had maintained his position his judgment would have been too damaging to Udomo. And Abrahams cannot stand this. So Mabi has to be subjected not only to Udomo's jeers but to his own inner doubts which border on impotence.

On learning of Udomo's death he writes to Lois:

It's nearly five years ago now since I last wrote you telling you of the death of Mhendi and asking if

I might come to you. Your silence was my answer then. Your silence may be my answer again. I'll understand. I did betray our friendship by going back when Udomo called. The trouble was that this call was also the call of Africa. But in the end I betrayed even that when I couldn't face up to its logic, spelled out in the death of Mhendi.

I don't think I wrote you anything about that last interview I had with him. I was too filled with passion and hatred. I can think back more calmly now. I remember he jeered at me after all his efforts to make me stay had failed. He called me 'Mr Moral Mabi' and mocked at my brand of squeamish patriotism. I think he and Mendhi were the only two who knew the price of what had to be done. And he was the only one among us prepared to pay it. Tom couldn't face the reality of Africa today, so he came back here and died a broken man within a month of his return. But of all of us I think I've been the most useless, the most ineffectual. I betrayed everybody and everything: You, Mhendi, Africa, yes, and Udomo and my art as well. He told me at that last interview that Mhendi wouldn't want to be mourned by me. I think he was right. It was another way of saying I was no good, for all my fine sentiments. Is it an attempt at self-justification or excuse if I say so, now that it's too late anyway, that an artist would make a mess of anything except being an artist? I don't know.[8]

Mabi's new-found humility rings as false as his attempt to point out the failure of morality within the African context. He seems to be merely echoing the dictum that politics is a dirty game. Otherwise it is difficult to see how Mabi has betrayed his art, except if he means that he should not have allowed himself to be involved in politics in the first instance, and should have kept his detachment. Has he betrayed Africa because he has refused to acquiesce in the selling of a friend? The moral alternatives which confront Udomo are simply not as compelling as he makes them out to be, although he works himself into a river of tears in thinking that his life-work will be jeopardised if he does not sacrifice his friend. Mabi's self-deprecating judgment that an artist would make a mess of anything except being an artist thus assumes an ironic over-tone, for Abrahams the artist makes a mess of what he does not fully understand. He does not—indeed, cannot—fully understand tribalism, but for him it remains the demon that must be exorcised at all costs.

Abrahams does not consider colonialism the anathema that it has generally been taken to be by most black writers. For him whatever evils it might have brought the black man are more than offset by the single blessing of having freed him from the evils of tribalism. Abrahams, like most African writers, is aware of the conflict between Westernism and tradition within most educated Africans. In an essay entitled *The Conflict of Cultures in Africa*, written two years before *A Wreath* was published, he singled out the novel, *Blanket Boy's Moon*, among the spate of books published on Africa in the previous year, because in spite of being a work of fiction, it 'still retains its validity as a serious attempt to throw light on what is, to my mind, the most pressing problem of Africa today: the problem of Africa's transition from the tribal past into the technological present'.[9] Abrahams does not really understand the nature of tribalism, which invariably he equates with the past. In *A Wreath* he postulates the well-known hypothesis that tribalism is a threat to national unity and will easily promote the growth of dictatorship. But his main con-cern is that tribal loyalties will stifle the human personality and prevent the growth of the kind of individual enterprise that has done so much to promote Western civilisation. Because he himself is completely Westernised, Abrahams assumes too readily that every African should inevitably embrace Western-isation. He has very little sympathy for the traditional values of Africa and the human values of tribal life.

Abrahams' ignorance of the traditional society influences our final judgment of Udomo and indeed of all the African leaders of the first generation. Trapped men, not belonging in either the traditional African or the white world, they invite more of our pity than admiration; which is sad, for Abrahams wants us to admire them. The epitaph to the novel from Walt Whitman indicates the thrust of Abrahams' intentions:

> Did we think victory great?
> So it is—But now it seems to me, when it cannot
> be helped, that defeat is great, And that death and
> dismay are great.[10]

The key phrase is 'when it cannot be helped'; the situation in which Udomo and others find themselves is not without trappings of the tragic, but Abrahams turns it into pathos, because there is nothing inevitable about the fates of these people. So the epitaph of Udomo, sung by Mabi in his closing letter to Lois, rings false within the totality of the actions of the novel:

> I can't think of him now without respect and
> admiration, my dear. Yes, there was something
> terrible about him. But wasn't it the power that did
> things, that changes the face of the world? What he
> did cannot be undone. Surely that is his memorial and
> his justification, if any were needed.[11]

The feeling persists that Udomo will need justification for a long time because, not by his own fault but his creator's, he has grappled with a shadow—and lost.

The forces hovering over the destiny of Africa are embodied in two women, Lois and Selina. Udomo falls under Lois' influence in Europe and under Selina's in Africa, but finds it necessary to break with both—in the interests of Africa!—because their assistance increasingly turns to fetters. Lois types his papers in London, and seeks to entrap him in her mountain retreat in southern France, just as Selina supports the party newspaper at the critical moment in Queenstown, helps found the party, and finally seeks to bind Udomo with the 'non-fraternisation' policy. Yet, Lois is the more successful character, although not in the sense in which Mabi constantly remembers her in Africa, or Udomo whispers to all his former London comrades: 'She still lingers,' which is Abrahams' way of saying that the flame of freedom of the mind and the heart which Lois lit in England still glows in Africa. Lois lingers because she is a spirit—an illusion, perhaps—and for the same reason she is more successful as a character than Selina, for Abrahams does not attempt to present her more than she is—a spirit. Paul Mabi and Udomo who worship her realise her quintessential nature, and worship her, not in body, but in spirit.

What Lois represents is repeatedly trumpeted in the course of the story but no more successfully than in those closing pages when Mabi communicates to her the news of Udomo's death, and thereby manages to paint an enduring portrait of their common friend:

> I don't think he ever forgot you. I think what you gave him in the months you shared was more important than either you or he realised. Perhaps he realised it towards the end. I had hints of that.
>
> I can't tell you why I have this impulse to defend his memory now. But the impulse is strong.
>
> But you and I, were we right with our private moralities? Can a man betray love and friendship, the gods we worship, and still be good? I think you'll still say no. Then how explain Udomo? I know the wrong he did you and Mhendi. But I also know the good he did Africa. Was he a good man? A great man? And is greatness beyond good and evil? Oh how he grows on me as I think ...
>
> Please write, Lois dear. We are the only two left. End the long silence. I wonder if tomorrow's Africans will understand the price at which their freedom was bought, and the share of it non-Africans like you had to pay. Write, my dear. Tell me I can come and lay in the sun with you and dream as we dreamed before Udomo came and brought reality into our lives. *Write, love.* [12]

The anxiety to re-establish contact only reminds us of the series of betrayals that run through the novel—of individuals and of causes. It reminds us of the isolation with which the book begins and in which the characters dwell. Lois, going on forty, lonely, meets Udomo in a bar, lonely, poor and cold. Soon, Udomo, using Lois' apartment, becomes the centre of the London group, holding all Africans together by his energy and dedication, whilst Lois brings everyone—white and

black, the governors and the governed—together at her parties. It is this world of reaching out to one another that the
betrayals, or the realities of African politics, intrude upon. The
part which whites like Lois play is to inject Western ideals,
especially personal freedom, into the African revolution.

The antithesis between Lois and Selina represents that
between Western ideals, of which Abrahams approves,
and tribalism which he roundly condemns. The successful
portrayal of Lois is balanced by Abrahams' failure with Selina.
Since he does not know tribalism or tribal life Abrahams
could hardly be expected to portray the tribal man or woman
successfully. So it is a fortunate omission that we don't see
them as individuals—perhaps Abrahams' way of illustrating
the lack of individuality of tribal life—just a mass of people.
Selina is a flat character. During his brief visit to Ghana,
Abrahams must have seen, and heard about the exploits of, the
so-called 'mammy traders', the retail traders who influenced
the direction of politics all over the West African coastal
region, although they were most successful in Ghana where
they played no small part in bringing Kwame Nkrumah to
power.

Within the development of the plot of *A Wreath* Udomo
turns to Selina and the women for help after the chiefs, the
traders and the intellectuals had failed him, each group more
concerned with its own interests than in their country's political emancipation. So Selina and the women are the only group
with the will and money, but even more important the influence and the organisation to help Udomo. Obviously their
role is that of a foil to the chiefs and elders. When Mabi objects
to Selina as 'a tribal woman', Adebhoy replies: 'We are a tribal
nation. Without Selina we couldn't have defeated the Council
of Chiefs and Elders.'[13] It is an uneasy alliance right from the
beginning. But it is plausible, and has in fact been proved time
and again all over colonial Africa, that it is possible to bind
essentially different people together in unity against the colonial ruler—until some measure of self-government is won,
after which divisions which had been papered over during the
struggle against the common foe come to the surface.

What is difficult to believe is the role Selina plays here.
Abrahams gives her more power than a woman, no matter

how wealthy, would normally assume within the traditional society. Selina as a blancophobe (the result of a brief visit to London) is no more credible than Selina the only power broker within Panafrica. As was the case with Leah in *Mine Boy*, Abrahams' creation runs away from him, and what started as a human being—no matter how unusual—soon becomes an ogress, ordering all the men (including her husband) about, blustering here and threatening there, forcing the non-fraternisation policy on the party and wrenching from Udomo a promise not to marry a white woman. Selina as the mother of the race (whenever we see her she is either carrying a baby or breast-feeding another) soon becomes a chief hustler, procuring young women for Udomo, Mhendi, and (of all people!) Lanwood; somehow she forgot Mabi. The practice is no more typically African than the woman who engages in it represents African womanhood.

Most of the faults of *A Wreath* come from the fact that Abrahams is looking at traditional African society through western eyes. Much of the description of the people and their customs—indeed of the country—seems to come from travel brochures. For example, the description of Queenstown, capital of Panafrica, written over several pages, shows that in spite of a (thin) veneer of modernisation—namely tarred roads, a large departmental store, three cinemas, and a big cathedral—the town has essentially preserved its traditional character. The point is not to dispute the truth of what Abrahams has seen and recorded; any visitor to a West African town would see perhaps more. Yet in a way Abrahams sees more than any visitor would see—because he looks with the eyes of the anthropologist or sociologist. The constant reference to 'two, three thousand years ago' is enough to point this out, and shows that Abrahams is still looking at traditional African society through the historical lens that produced *Wild Conquest*. In *A Wreath* he has recorded fairly well things he saw during his visit; it is when he writes about things he did not see that imagination, never one of Abrahams' strongest faculties, plays him false.

What, for example, could be more banal than the launching of the African Freedom Party, or the reception of the London group when later they arrive to join Udomo, now freed from prison and made Prime Minister, in nation-building? Coming to *A Wreath* from *Wild Conquest* we can easily put our finger on what is wrong. Abrahams is in the realm of 'don't-know' and has to use his imagination, or historical sense. Once again that sense has played him false. The reception party is a historical pageant. The scene is nowhere in Africa, but is more credible as a Roman procession in the time of the Caesars, complete with togas (the Ghanaian *kente* cloth is close enough to the Roman toga) Whenever Abrahams pictures events beyond his knowledge it is such historical pageantry that leaps forward, as in the description of the canoemen who take Mhendi across the lake on his first journey into Pluralia:

> A long, slender, shapely canoe awaited them on the edge of the lake. It was manned by six of the most beautifully shaped men Mhendi had ever seen. The leader beckoned them impatiently. They got in. The leader pushed against the bank till the canoe's nose pointed towards the mountains. He grunted once. The canoe shot away. The men picked up rhythm, their bodies moved in unison, their blades as one. In ... Out ... In ... Out ... In ... Out ... In ... Out ... In ... Out ... In ... Out ... In ... Out ... The slender craft sped across the dark water. The men moved with an easy, tireless rhythm.
>
> 'You must be very hungry, Maria,' Mhendi said.
>
> The leader of the canoeists spoke harshly.
>
> 'He says you are not to speak,' Maria said. 'He says the sound of speech turned his men's attention from the rhythm of their work and the boat goes slower.'
>
> 'I'm sorry,' Mhendi said.
>
> In ... Out ... In ... Out ...
>
> Mhendi's stomach rumbled. His throat felt dry and swollen. From an almost deep purple, Maria's lips had turned an ashy white. She kept on wetting them. Mhendi wanted to comfort her. If her thirst were half as great as his, if her hunger half as great as his, then she must be in agony. They had not eaten a proper meal since midday yesterday. And now it was going on to midday again. Eating on the

bumping truck in the swirling dust had been impossible. You've grown soft, Mhendi, he told himself. Poor Maria. No need for her to suffer this. Pluralia means nothing to her. He took her hand.

In ... Out ... In ... Out ...

They were the only people on the great lake. For all the signs of life they might as well be lost in a slender boat on the vast ocean that covers so much of the earth's surface. But there were the mountains ahead; and they gave comfort.

In ... Out ... In ... Out ...

Were these men human? Could ordinary mortals keep up this machine-like rhythm hour after hour?

The sun climbed to a point overhead, stayed there, then moved westward. Mhendi began to feel light-headed. Maria seemed in a daze where he could not reach her. His father had, as a young man, performed feats of endurance such as these canoeists now did. Men in the tribal state could still do this. Then the machine-age caught up with them. But what of the uglier side of tribalism? What of its greatest crime: the stifling and destroying of the human personality? That's what Udomo is up against as I'll never be in Pluralia. Win or lose, my people are at least a century ahead of his. My God! I wouldn't be in his shoes for anything. In ... Out ... In ... Out ...[14]

This passage points out a major difference between Abrahams and most black African writers who celebrate the superiority of the traditional man over his descendants. In contrast, Abrahams glorifies Mhendi the modern African, product of Westernisation (whom Abrahams knows because the feelings of both the author and his creation are the same), at the expense of the canoeists, 'men in the tribal state', with their primeval energy. To Mhendi they are savages, emblem of the evil energy of the African past—the emphasis is on their brawn and, correspondingly, their lack of sense. 'Were these men human? Could ordinary mortals keep up this machine-like rhythm hour after hour?' So had another character observed of the Matabele warriors in *Wild Conquest*. Indeed, it is difficult to escape the feeling that Abrahams had material left over from the earlier novel which he felt reluctant to throw away.

An evidence is the death-scene of Udomo, which competes with the most melodramatic scene of witch-hunting in *Wild Conquest*. The power of the drum on the tribal man connotes the hold that ritualism still has over him. Even Udomo is enchanted, and is freed only by the terrible pain of one of his assailants' knives. 'For a terrible moment he was a man again.' This scene should indicate how much Udomo set out to do—free a whole people from darkness. Indeed, in true Frankenstein manner he confronts the monsters he has raised: he is hacked to death by the two men who had always acted as his guard; but to show their reversion to tribalism they have removed their party garments and are smeared only in juju paints. The melodramatic end, in which not only the participants but the whole of Africa collapse in a trance-like peacefulness attests to the power of the evil forces. 'And the night was quiet over Africa. The moon was up. The stars shone brightly in the silent night.'[15] Thus Abrahams aims to show that Udomo's death is not a surrender to darkness; the people of Panafrica can see more clearly now for the evil forces have worked themselves out, making Udomo's death a sacrifice in more than one sense—his own deliberate sacrifice for Africa's progress, and the tribesmen's sacrifice to their gods.

Michael Udomo is a true Abrahams hero in that, beginning from typically restrictive circumstances he widens his vision and transcends his narrow background. Udomo is a very typical figure, but he comes across very forcefully (more so than any of Abrahams' characters) because this time Abrahams has a personality (Nkrumah's), a political programme (The Convention Peoples Party's), and the story of a particular country (The Gold Coast) as his model. His essay, *The Conflict of Cultures in Africa* shows how heavily he has drawn on these sources. But, then, both Nkrumah's background and much of what happened in the Gold Coast were duplicated in the rest of the continent.

To Udomo, political independence is only a means; the task confronting the black African nations is 'to make the greatest transition from the past to the present'.[16] Tribalism symbolises this past. 'We need to build up national loyalties as against tribal loyalties,' he intones. 'Otherwise we'll never build a strong African state that is as modern as any of the European states. Before Africa's voice will be listened to in the world, we need strong modern States.'[17] Udomo is so convinced that tribalism is an unmitigated evil that he readily sacrifices almost everything in order to defeat it. Realising the realities of power in a tribal nation, he allies with tribalism (represented by Selina) in order to accomplish his political revolution; for the success of the more important task of freeing his people from the past, he readily betrays his best friend. 'Personal relationships must be subordinated to the struggle. Only the fight is important.'[18] It is a slogan whose full implications were not understood by the Africans who uttered it in the dreamland of London. When they confront the realities of Africa, even Mabi flees, for the logic of the slogan takes the African nationalist into sinister companies. Udomo makes a pact with white racists and betrays his best friend in order to obtain the technical aid which he needs to propel his country from the tribal past to the technological present.

As to the fate of the first generation of African leaders Abrahams had only his intuition to guide him when he wrote his novel in 1954–55. The political tight-rope which Udomo has to walk between the traditionalists in his Cabinet and the white racists at his borders makes his fall inevitable. But his destruction by the forces within his own gates is truly prophetic, for Abrahams demonstrates through the fate of Udomo—and Nkrumah's fall has confirmed this—that the African leader who leads his people to political freedom may be prevented by his own countrymen from stimulating them to progress.

> You can guess the reason for his murder. They wanted to go back to the days of tribal glory. You know there are people all over the world, white as well as black, who are attracted to tribalism. Among other things it has security, colour, and emotional outlets that the bleak, standardised, monotonous

chromium and neon benefits of mass-production civilisation lack. You know also there are many, mainly among the whites, who say that the trouble in Africa today is due to the fact that Africans have moved away from tribalism too rapidly. They are foolish people who don't understand the true nature of tribalism. Udomo did. He worked against it, quietly, secretly at first and then, as recent accounts of developments there show, more boldly, more openly. And so he had to be hacked to pieces in true tribal tradition.[19]

Abrahams portrays Udomo as a giant, for he has single-handedly attempted to change the destiny of a whole nation. For Abrahams, the final *rationale* for Udomo's betrayal of Mhendi is that the cause of political freedom in Pluralia is secondary to that of spiritual freedom in Panafrica, for as both white and black characters repeatedly assert, the blacks in Pluralia have left the ways of the tribe behind, and are at least a hundred years ahead of the tribal people of Panafrica.

Abrahams minimises the significance of Mhendi's death to the movement he leads by mercifully allowing his followers to escape. Equally important, Udomo's opponents cannot undo the good work he has accomplished. 'You know it won't make any difference,' Mhendi defiantly tells his captors, 'They will be free.'[20] This is balanced by Udomo's defiance of Selina and Adebhoy: 'You're too late, my friends. You're too late . . .'[21] And his enemies bitterly agree. 'They'd given him too much time. The great machine of progress was in motion now: didn't really even need him any more for its wheels to go round. They were too late.'[22] As the 'authorial' character Mabi puts it in his final assessment of Udomo's achievements: 'they were too late. He'd carried things too far forward for them to be able to put the clock back now.'[23] So, in spite of his death, Udomo has launched traditional Africa on an irreversible voyage towards spiritual freedom.

NOTES

[1] *A Wreath for Udomo* (Faber and Faber, London, 1956). All page references are to this edition.

[2] *Ibid.*, p. 39.

[3] *Ibid.*, p. 57.

[4] *Ibid.*, pp. 122–3.

[5] *Ibid.*, p. 283.

[6] *Ibid.*, p. 289.

[7] *Ibid.*, pp. 228–9.

[8] *Ibid.*, pp. 307–8.

[9] *International Affairs*, XXX:3 (July, 1954), p. 304.

[10] Whitman, 'To a Foil'd European Revolutionaire', in *Complete Poetry and Selected Prose and Letters*, ed. E. Holloway (Nonesuch Press, London, 1938).

[11] *A Wreath for Udomo*, p. 308.

[12] *Ibid.*, p. 309.

[13] *Ibid.*, p. 266.

[14] *Ibid.*, pp. 215–17.

[15] *Ibid.*, p. 306.

[16] *Ibid.*, p. 255.

[17] *Ibid.*, p. 203.

[18] *Ibid.*, p. 45.

[19] *Ibid.*, p. 308.

[20] *Ibid.*, p. 288.

[21] *Ibid.*, p. 302.

[22] *Ibid.*, p. 303.

[23] *Ibid.*, p. 308.

Chapter Eight

A Night of Their Own

In spite of the nine years that separate them, *A Night of Their Own*[1] is a natural sequence to *A Wreath for Udomo*. The Pluralia in the earlier novel (which is South Africa thinly disguised) takes the centre stage, and the problems and attitudes hinted at variously in *A Wreath* are dramatised in *A Night*. The white racists of South Africa, like the tribesmen of Panafrica, need to be reminded that Western culture is a world culture, not 'reserved for Europeans only':

> The true motive forces of Western culture are to be found in the first place in the teachings of the Christ who taught a new concept of men's relations with their God and with each other, a concept that cuts across tribal gods and tribal loyalties and embraces all men in all lands offering them a common brotherhood. From this primary source flow all its other motive forces in philosophy and the arts. The Kantian ethical theory, the Rights of Man, democracy and the uniquely new status it offers individual man, all form part of the non-exclusive sources of Western culture. From them stem the great advances in science and material prosperity, in man's mastery of the dark corners of the world in which he lives. To deny this fundamental outwardness in its nature is to deny Western culture itself. This denial has, I think, been largely made by the whites of the multi-racial societies up to now.[2]

Thus apartheid, like tribalism, stands accused because of its exclusiveness. Rather than surrender any part of their power and privilege the whites in South Africa have rejected the values underlying Western culture, and have deliberately set their faces against a situation which holds the best possibility for unreserved association between the races. The blacks in the country form the largest group of urbanised and detribalised black men and women on the continent and have accepted the moral and ethical bases of Western culture more completely than Africans in any of the other territories, with the possible exception of the black élite of the French African colonies. 'The result is that it is the black leaders of the African National Congress who are today fighting in defence of the moral and ethical assumptions underlying Western culture.'[3]

In an angry letter to London's *The Times* in 1956 where he defended Father Trevor Huddleston who had been accused of fomenting trouble in South Africa, Abrahams warned of the danger posed to the existence of the Commonwealth by the oppressive policies of the South African government.[4] The following year South Africa was expelled from the Commonwealth, largely through the opposition of the newly independent African nations. *A Night* applauds this political ostracism as a fitting retribution for the country's flouting of the Commonwealth ideal, and a pointer to her moral isolation from the rest of the world. Since 1956 when *A Wreath* was published, events in Africa had moved so fast that being black had ceased to be a burden. In West and North Africa, there is no disadvantage even in being an Indian. But while the rest of the world is moving forward South Africa is journeying in the opposite direction, its policies motivated by fear. 'The things they do, they do out of a fear that has grown so great that it has become a thing of evil.'[5]

The nature of this evil is explored at length in *A Night*. How palpable the darkness has become can be seen when we compare Abrahams' earlier picture of South Africa with what he saw during his second visit. In *Song of the City*, published barely three years after Abrahams left the country, we see the extent of the record kept by the government on the non-whites,[6] but *A Night* shows how frighteningly comprehensive it has become. The army of informants, the elaborate system of deception and suspicion, human beings living like ants with all the warning systems of ants, and the comprehensiveness of the record kept on *everyone* by the government, all in the determination to conserve white power, presage the tyranny of Big Brother. Abrahams' point, repeatedly stated to the point of monotony, is that government interference in individual lives now threatens both white and black: increasingly all over the land young people of all races have to mature much too quickly, and therefore much too artificially; everything is forced so hard as to destroy their humanity. 'Soon this land and all its people, black, brown, white, and what will you, soon they will all be strangers to the meaning of compassion: the trend is there, sharp and clear, unmistakable.'[7] If the present trend continues, South Africa will one day produce a race of men who will only feel and respond in accordance with the dictates of time and place; 'then we will see the day when the world becomes a really ugly, scientific and brutal thing'.[8] Thus, Abrahams gives a universal dimension to the situation in South Africa:

> This has nothing to do with mobs or God's colour or even colour. It has to do with tyranny, with oppression, with human cruelty: all the things minorities have always done throughout history when they have tried to hold power against the will of the majorities. And now, here, in our time, the issues have been reduced to the basic conflict between good and evil ... There is no hope of any good any more in white rule. No hope of good. And when there is no hope of good, then the evil is complete.[9]

Abrahams is deeply disturbed by the black man's response to this evil, and addresses himself to the black population of South Africa. The book carries the dedication:

For
my friends
WALTER SISULU
and
NELSON MANDELA
and all the others,
the captured and the still free,
who are at war against the evils
of this night of their own.

Abrahams' fear is that the black South African risks contamination by the disease he is fighting, for he is increasingly demeaning himself by becoming as colour conscious as his white oppressors. For example, not long ago, all the people who opposed the colour bar were united in the multi-national African National Congress and were committed to a policy of non-violence; now, control of the Congress has been seized by an extremist group, *poqo*, composed entirely of black men, dedicated to a policy of open terror and claiming 'that nobody could help the Africans win their salvation and they did not need anybody's help'.[10] Perhaps more terrifying, the black masses have welcomed with undisguised enthusiasm the stand of the new group.

In *Dark Testament, Song of the City,* and *The Path of Thunder* Abrahams has taken pains to point out the special place occupied by the Jews in bridging the gulf between black and white. But when he visited South Africa in 1952 he could hardly find a good white in the country, and his bitterness was directed at all the whites. 'In the dictionary of values of White South Africans,' he concluded, 'it is better that democracy and all its ethical and moral bases perish rather than that the present power relationship between Black and White be upset.'[11] The only rays of hope which Abrahams found in this depressing gloom filtered through the Indians, and his enthusiasm about their activities more than counterbalanced his depression about the whites. As he recorded in *Tell Freedom,* Abrahams had known of Indian anti-apartheid activities even before he left the country in 1939. When he arrived in Durban on his way out, he was already familiar with the efforts of the younger Indians, the Liberal Study Group, who 'welcomed me as one of their own'.[12] As he went about the country in 1952, Abrahams noticed that the campaign against apartheid was getting under way, in which all non-whites were united against white supremacy. 'Indeed, the Indians are, viewed with the perspective of history, integrating themselves more successfully into the shape of a future South Africa without racial tensions than the Whites.'[13]

As is to be expected from a writer who is not particularly gifted with imagination, a lot that Abrahams saw in the Indian locations during his visit in 1952 found its way into *A Night,* often only thinly disguised: the poverty and misery in which most Indians lived in Durban which made Abrahams' slum childhood in Johannesburg seem heaven by comparison; the character of Dr Dawood Nunkhoo in the novel which is almost literally copied from Abrahams' description of the personality of Dr Yusuf Mohamed Dadoo, founder of the South African Indian Congress. The South African Indians are Abrahams' example of a people living and fighting on the highest level of freedom. In spite of black hostility, which has manifested itself in two race riots heavily destructive of Indian lives and property, the Indian leaders have remained committed to the idea of majority rule in South Africa. This is all the more significant because, while the present is dark enough, there is no certainty that the future will be kinder to the Indians. On the contrary, black rule may be more oppressive than the white rule against which they are fighting. For the Africans the promise of the end of white rule is clear in its meaning; the Indian has no assurance that he would, at the very least, be free of racial indignity. It is a tribute to the nobility of the human spirit that under such circumstances the Indians can still throw themselves whole-heartedly into the fight against apartheid; in fact, they have to beg the embittered black leadership to be allowed to make their contribution to the struggle.

Politically, Indian participation in the resistance is very important in terms of Abrahams' vision of the future of the plural societies: he would have deemed it too ominous for the future to leave the fight against apartheid in the hands of blacks alone. Indian participation in the struggle bodes well for the future of South Africa and all plural societies. It does not mean that Abrahams foresees a time when all racial distinctions will vanish:

> I don't think there will ever be a time like that. I think there will always be or, at least for as far into the future as matters to us—Indians and Europeans and Africans. Each will tend to want to stay within its own group. And there is nothing wrong with that. What I hope is that each group will accept and respect the equal humanity of the other.[14]

Will such a day ever dawn? Implicit in the title of the book is the conviction that it will. The background of the 'night' during which Abrahams wrote *A Night* was the South African government's success in cracking the backbone of the African underground movement in 1963–64. Summing up after his visit in 1952, Abrahams had written: 'But the change will come. That much I saw when I was there.'[15] In 1964, the gathering forces in the anti-apartheid movement on which he based his optimism had been smashed, and Abrahams must have felt that the Africans (and perhaps he himself) needed to be reassured that this night would not last forever, and indeed would be followed by a glorious dawn.

Abrahams does not shut his ears to the bad news, but takes comfort in the fact that change is a part of nature, a belief which prevents him from voicing the type of despair very common among black South African writers. 'Because there are no stars in the sky,' intones a character in this novel, 'is no reason for us to assume that darkness is eternal.'[16] True, as all the leaders of the underground recognise, it is not simply the fact of daylight that is important, for we ought to be concerned about the kind of daylight that will follow the darkness, but there must be a clear knowledge that there will be daylight—or life will be impossible. *A Night* closes on this note of affirmation, even as the forces of the underground flee the country:

> ... And so our men must leave us. Some to die; some to go into prison; some to hide; some to go to far lands. And we must be alone in the land, waiting and working and fighting and scheming for the day of reunion, the day that must follow this terrible night.
> ... Perhaps Dawood will not be there at that morning of reunion; perhaps *he* will not be there; perhaps I will not be there. For there will be many, many casualties before that morning comes. Sammy Naidoo and an army of others fallen in battle will not be there, but it is important that their spirit, that what they lived and died for, be there. For that morning will come: a good morning after the terrors of this night. It is for this that Sammy died; for this that they have slipped across the sky-line of the sea; for this that we must do many things, endure many things, and see our men leave.[17]

For Abrahams the promise of dawn is more than a hope; it is a certainty, an irrevocable part of nature. The present fighters may not be there in the morning but it is essential that their spirit should. If daylight means merely to be alive, then there will be no need to fight, for that too is a part of the natural order, beyond the control of any man. It is precisely because it means more than that, because it means living on the highest plane, that the Indians are fighting against apartheid in South Africa, fighting to bring about a government run by the black majority. The blacks too must not lose sight of their own goal, for in fighting for their own freedom, they are fighting on behalf of the whole of mankind. Says the hero of *A Night*:

> It isn't the fact of birth or death that is most significant. It is the fact of living. Being alive, being human is more important than being either Indian or black or white or South African... All I am saying is that the point of these slogans of yours, the point of my being here, the point of the risks we all take is to create a South Africa in which it is possible for us to live and grow and feel like people. All of us.[18]

The tone of the novel is uncompromisingly noble and determinedly serious, making the characters' gestures as stagey as their dialogues. But the cumulative effect is powerful. We are appalled to think of a people to whom the reality of day-to-day living is so horrible that they are forced to try to keep it at arm's length with incantations such as this. It is only those who have won their battles who can afford to contemplate the truth of what went on while they were being fought. In this novel there is very little agonising over means and ends as in *A Wreath*, for we are no longer faced with a generation in transition who have to make the cruellest choice, the choice between two evils; now it is a generation at war with perhaps the greatest evil that has confronted mankind, and the choice becomes painfully easy.

> Nunkhoo turned to Nkosi. 'The means-and-ends argument is pretty wonderful as long as it remains an argument: it assumes that issues are either right or

wrong, that the choice is always a straightforward one between good and evil. But the moment you enter the field of action this simplification of values falls away. Nearly always, in situations like this one, an action is at once both right and wrong, is charged with the possibility of both good and evil. The real problem here, the real gamble, the real hope is that our judgement has been sufficiently sound, our faith in the phantasies sufficiently strong for our actions to tip the scales in favour of good. That is the limit of our guarantee: a mere hope that out of our action will come good rather than evil. Because this has not been enough for many people, they have chosen inaction. One does not risk being wrong or doing evil if one does nothing.'

'I quarrel with none of this,' Nkosi said. 'You know that and you know the nature of my quarrel—at least I think you do.'

'That often in the process of fighting evil you adopt—'

'Or you are forced to adopt—'

'Or are forced to adopt methods that are as evil as the evil you fight. My answer is that if the ultimate objective is a good one, that is as much as we can ask of any cause. Beyond that, each man makes his own private choice. And here, in South Africa today, the choice has been made painfully simple.'[19]

It is necessary to Abrahams' vision of the ultimate goal of the underground that it is a black man who raises the moral questions, in a cause in which Indian leaders willingly lay down their lives. Richard Nkosi (real name Richard Dube) is the custodian of the conscience of the revolution, a fact underlined by the Indians' recognition that their future will be guaranteed if such a man is in the saddle when the morning dawns. On the face of it, Nkosi is the Black Pimpernel whose mission is not to smuggle out the enemies of the regime but to smuggle in the money that would enable the underground to continue the fight. But his symbolic importance is not lost on the authorities who mount the widest police search in the history of the country to catch him—nor is it lost on himself: 'I have just borrowed the name, as others have before me, and as others will after me, because the name has now been turned into the spirit and the will of the resistance. It is a symbol now.'[20] Obviously Abrahams thinks an artist would best serve his purpose as a representative of that symbol, and for the conception of Nkosi we do not need to go beyond the portrayal of Paul Mabi in *A Wreath*, of whom he is a carbon-copy, even to the details of their physical appearances. Like Mabi, Nkosi too has very sharp and observant eyes, and is extremely detached. Dee, soon to become emotionally tangled with him, sums him up: 'Uncommitted, detached, objective—any of these words will do,' meaning, as she explains further, that 'you react and respond with the kind of self-assurance that is not common to us—all of us—who are non-Europeans in this country.'[21]

To Nkosi the mission had started as a swashbuckling expedition, but he soon learns that action means commitment, and thus strikes a theme which reverberates throughout the novel, that each of us is his brother's keeper. Abrahams explicitly brings out this theme by dragging in Captain Stikkelund, a man who had lost the capacity to believe, so that Nkosi can effect his escape and the idea he represents may not be destroyed. Captain Stikkelund spirits away Nkosi and Dr Nunkhoo, refusing to take money for his services because in his own words 'every man must take some responsibility for every other man'.[22] The captain's effort not only saves the underground, but is also self-regenerative; Nkosi's running away, Stikkelund sums up, is not a defeat, but an act of faith—which enables himself to rediscover his capacity to believe:

> The Captain thought: how often through the cen-
> turies have men gone through this self-same pattern
> of action, this escape from tyranny in order to resist
> it? They had to carry a little child out of a land once
> to escape the wrath and fear of a king. This is as old as
> time and man, and it is an honour for a man like me,
> who has lost his capacity to believe, to make contact
> with this brand of faith once more...[23]

Captain Stikkelund's recollection of the story of the child smuggled out of the country in order to save him from the anger of a king has biblical overtones—so Christ was smuggled out of Bethlehem to save him from the anger of Herod. Nkosi is a messianic figure. His mission to smuggle money into the country of course physically saves the underground, just as his symbolic importance saves their morale. But he performs this task on the individual level, too. Nkosi, the artist-as-saviour, saves Dawood, for the latter would have been arrested during the police raid in Johannesburg but for the fact that he was busy in Natal attending to Nkosi's welfare and so could not attend the Johannesburg meeting. Spiritually, Nkosi elevates Dicky Naicker, the young Indian who remains in the underground because Sammy his mentor impresses on him that for the sake of Indian survival it is necessary to make a common cause with the blacks. Nkosi's love for the Indian girl, Dee, enables Dicky to transcend his narrow racial outlook, and he thinks there is a future for all races in South Africa—if a man like Nkosi leads the black movement. Nkosi saves the reactionary Old Man Nanda from the latter's blinding attachment to material wealth, gives a spiritual dimension to the old man's life, and succeeds thereby in uniting the estranged father and son. 'It struck him that it was because of this little black man that he was closer to his son now than he had been since the boy became a man.'[24]

This theme of the 'divine', or at any rate, more-than-human, mission of the artist is best seen in Nkosi's relationship with Dee Nunkhoo, the Indian cripple whose physical deformity is only an emblem of a psychological deformity. Nkosi, by painting Dee in her new flush of happiness and love, elevates her out of her dullness and dreariness by the wand of his magic; he heals, reveals to her her own capacity for joy and wonder, makes her 'see' for the first time. She tells him: 'I've seen all this so often but I'm only really seeing it now. I think it was those sketches of yours. I suddenly saw just *how* beautiful this place, and this country, really are.'[25] Nkosi saves her from her sordid past, and reveals to her the true joys of love, thus giving a new direction to her life. To her brother she explains the importance Nkosi has brought into her life:

Even if he died ... I'd be in the most awful mess ... But it won't be like before ... I'll always know where I'm going and what is right. It is like knowing your way through the jungle. You may not get through, that is chance, but you know the way and you know that whatever happens you can't get lost. I hope we get through—I'd love to have his children...[26]

The regenerative love between Dee and Nkosi (and its potential fruition, as is shown in Dee's longing to have his children) is meant to be a contrast to the love between Karl Van As and Mildred Scott, which after thirteen years comes to an abrupt end, condemning both to a future of loneliness and despair, because the cowardly Karl, like Van der Merwe in *Song of the City*, is afraid to put his career in jeopardy, and has therefore chosen to safeguard his professional future, instead of following the dictates of his heart and living on the highest plane, as a human being, like his great ancestor. Karl is 'the real descendant of the voortrekker Paul Van As and his wife Elsie, who had been with the small honoured band that had gone forth to conquer a wild land and had laid the foundations of this nation with their blood and their sacrifice'.[27] But Karl's cowardly behaviour contrasts with the courage of his ancestor, and illustrates Abrahams' theme of the deterioration of idealism in South Africa. Karl claims he does not like apartheid but goes along because of what he conceives to be his duty to his people: 'You don't just turn your back on your people because they are marching to disaster,'[28] intones this time-server in words which would make his ancestor squirm in his grave. The rest of Karl's life will be terrible, for he has deliberately chosen to dwell on the plain while the mountain is within his grasp:

He thought for a while and then his words came out with a careful delicacy. 'You can't walk alone. Many have given the illusion but none have really walked alone. Man is not made that way. Each man is bedded in his people, in their history and their culture and their values ... And so each man wants and works, almost automatically, for the approval of his people ... When a man believes his people are taking the wrong turning, it becomes difficult. If you're a Jan Hofmeyr, you stand up and you speak your mind and you live and die with the burden of being rejected by your own people. But we're not all cast in the mould. There are people who cannot bear the burden, so they do not stand up ...'[29]

Karl may be the most obvious but he is not the only link between *A Night* and *Wild Conquest*. In the heat of 1963–64 when most of the novel was written Abrahams had little time for subtle characterisation. The copious use of his notes from his visit of 1952 is a case in point; another is the use of a formula which he had employed—with disastrous results—in *Wild Conquest*. As in the Matabele section of that novel, Abrahams is here more interested in the ideas that his characters represent, and there is very little attempt to make individuals of them. Nkosi, as has been pointed out, is a duplicate of Paul Mabi. As in *Wild Conquest*, characters seem to have been coupled together, even if it is a coupling of opposites, so as to save time. Take for instance, Dr Dawood Nunkhoo and Sammy Naidoo, leaders of the Natal branch of the underground:

> (Nunkhoo) was tall, pale-skinned, graceful. A thick mop of wavy, jet-black hair crowned a handsome, humorous face. There were streaks of grey in the hair, but these only enhanced his appearance. The doctor looked what he was: a handsome upper-class Hindu of wealthy family who had had the best education Europe could offer and money could buy.
>
> In contrast, black Sammy Naidoo, big, burly, clumsy-looking, was obviously a descendant of those poor, low-class Indian peasants who were brought to the country as indentured coolie labour about the middle of the nineteenth century.[30]

It does not demand much effort to detect that in spite of the similarity in their views, Dawood and Sammy are exact opposites in every other respect—physical appearance, family background. Even the act of coupling the men in subsequent paragraphs betrays artistic tactlessness, and shows the desperate hurry in which Abrahams wrote, for surely he could have made a greater effort to conceal his framework. Every other character seems to have his double. Captain Stikkelund, an instinctively good man, albeit disillusioned with the world, is tall and thin and fair—the opposite in all respects of Old Man Nanda, his chief customer, for whose guiding principle of life he feels nothing but contempt. Then Abrahams seems to give the game away when, impatiently as it were, in apologising for the thinness of the Captain, and vouching for his honesty, he says, 'it's not what he looks like but what he is that's important'.[31] It is a truism which Abrahams must have been muttering to himself as he ticked off each character.

In spite of the failure of its characterisation and dialogue, *A Night* succeeds because Abrahams refreshingly casts his novel in the form of a dialectical, political fable in which the dilemmas facing the main groups are stated and dramatised, thus making the story exciting and gripping in spite of the fact that for a novel of action there is surprisingly little action. All the characters are forced to admit that South Africa is a moral jungle where there is no form of action left open which is legal on the one hand or humanely justifiable on the other. *A Night* is too simple as a novel, but succeeds as an explanatory fable about the fate of different races. Given the atmosphere of 1963–64 and Abrahams' purpose, the weaknesses of the novel are perhaps inevitable. Yet the achievement is considerable. The novel is largely free from self-conscious literariness and hyperboles, the besetting faults of novels on the same subject, such as Richard Rive's *Emergency* (1964). In spite of its political preoccupation, the story is remarkably clear, and the concise narrative does not stifle the anger and the anguish.

NOTES

[1] *A Night of Their Own* (Faber and Faber, London, 1965). All page references are to this edition.
[2] *The Conflict of Cultures in Africa*, p. 308, in *International Affairs* XXX:3.
[3] *Ibid.*, p. 309.
[4] *The Times*, May 10, 1956, p. 7.

[5] *A Wreath for Udomo*, p. 283.
[6] *Song of the City*, pp. 38–9.
[7] *A Night of Their Own*, p. 68.
[8] *Ibid.*, p. 87.
[9] *Ibid.*, p. 237.
[10] *Ibid.*, p. 60.
[11] *Return to Goli*, p. 176.
[12] *Tell Freedom*, p. 304.
[13] *Return to Goli*, p. 89.
[14] *Ibid.*, p. 96.
[15] *Ibid.*, p. 203.
[16] *Ibid.*, p. 89.
[17] *Ibid.*, p. 269.
[18] *Ibid.*, pp. 50–1.

[19] *Ibid.*, pp. 89–90.
[20] *Ibid.*, p. 249.
[21] *Ibid.*, p. 47.
[22] *Ibid.*, p. 260.
[23] *Ibid.*, p. 264.
[24] *Ibid.*, p. 253.
[25] *Ibid.*, p. 122.
[26] *Ibid.*, pp. 200–1.
[27] *Ibid.*, p. 153.
[28] *Ibid.*, p. 174.
[29] *Ibid.*, p. 172.
[30] *Ibid.*, p. 37.
[31] *Ibid.*, p. 255.

Chapter Nine

This Island Now

This Island Now[1] is the climax of Abrahams' examination of the ways in which the blacks hope to attain freedom and achieve their racial identity. Published barely a year after *A Night of Their Own*, its dominant mood is urgency, as the title of the book indicates well enough. Thus, although one might have assumed that Abrahams had been working on the novel and laid it aside in 1963–64 to write *A Night*, it appears that in fact most of *This Island Now* was not written until the earlier book was published. Either Abrahams was dissatisfied with the conclusions reached in the earlier novel or he found the problem too pressing to be dealt with in one book. Abrahams, never a good artist except when on familiar grounds, has transferred the setting from Africa to the West Indies where he now lives. There is no doubt that the physical terrain of *This Island Now* is largely that of Jamaica as described in his essay, *The Real Jamaica*, and the political terrain that of Haiti. Yet the book is a serious political novel precisely because it avoids the easy banalities that its theme and facile analogy with, say, Dr Duvalier might provoke.

The over-riding quality of *This Island Now* is its simplicity. It is partly an epic simplicity, the subject of the novel being the efforts of an individual to revolutionise the power structure of his society. In addition, it is a simplicity which allows the novel's political theme, free from the accretion of confusing details, to be transferred from its peculiar geographical setting. The problems which confront President Albert Josiah are more than those of a tiny island in the Caribbean; they are problems which face the developing countries in general and which have threatened to embroil the big powers in a global war. At the beginning of his revolution, Josiah threatens that if the foreign mercantile companies attempt to buck him, he will 'nationalise everything, beat the racialist drum, drive all capitalists out of the country, and ask for help from the communist world'.[2]

One effect of the novel's simplicity is the lack of any details of social living. More than in *A Night of Their Own*, Abrahams is so preoccupied with the political conflict that everything else recedes to the background. This includes the mass of the people. Society in *This Island Now* operates like an iceberg: a glittering speck dominates the landscape while the vast bulk remains invisible. True, the people are present throughout the novel, the continuity of their lives providing a kind of stable background, but they are largely mute, passive, and helpless; instead of forming a live background which will provide the plot with genuine action, they constitute the clay from which Josiah wants to mould a revolutionary society. What makes the conflicts within the novel so intense is that the stakes are so high: no less than the destiny of the three million people of the island and—beyond them, what we are never allowed to forget throughout the narrative—the fate of the whole black race.

Instead of the day-to-day continuities of social living Abrahams gives us glimpses of grassroot politics. During the previous regime, a class of disgruntled elements had gradually grown up, consisting mostly of those who failed their examinations and thus could not get into the vast, cumbersome and overstaffed public service. Their day-to-day lives consist of scrambling desperately not to sink back into 'the vast faceless mass' out of which they had tried to claw and fight their way. They were used—and despised—by the white and coloured upper classes, while the black mass of the islanders, either completely illiterate or semi-literate, envied and looked up to them. Describing them as 'symbols of the wasted manhood of the nation', Josiah makes these social rejects the corner-stone of his political revolution by using them as conduits between him and the people.

> Periodically small groups of key party people from
> the country areas came to the Palace to dine quietly
> with the President. The President used these small
> informal dinners to keep himself informed of the
> mood and problems of the country as seen through

the eyes of dedicated party workers on the spot. He also used them to send back to the party, and the country, explanations of policies and ideas for future action. At these parties the President asked questions, posed problems, and spoke more frankly about the things that were on his mind than he ever did to the nation at large. Neither parliament, the press nor the mercantile community had ever been able to get any information of precisely what was discussed at any of these dinners. All they knew was that Josiah and the mass of the people of the country seemed linked by a channel of communication and understanding, strong and sustaining as that between mother and child at the moment after birth before the cord is cut.[4]

The simplicity of *This Island Now* is most evident in its characterisation. There are no complexities of character. Each individual is used to represent a concept, usually the guiding principle of his profession. 'Cannibalism is part of business',[5] says Old Nathan Isaacs, the head of the Isaacs' family empire, as he closes his deal with Josiah. According to John Stanhope, the head of the civil service, 'no area of the life of a good public servant, especially a very senior one, could ever be wholly private or personal'.[6] Maxwell Johnson, the editor of the island's main newspaper, gives the classic interpretation of the journalist's duty: 'Our business is to get the news and when we go beyond the getting and presenting of the news then our so-called commitment goes to hell.'[7] Justice Wright, setting himself on a collision course with Josiah, intones: 'The rule of law must never depend on the strength or weakness of the position of any ruler. It must be constant, above person and position.'[8] There can be no real complexities where characters stand for and represent such sure and simple concepts as professional ethics.

Abrahams further simplifies the picture by dividing his characters into black and white—along racial lines. A critic has complained of Abrahams' 'infuriating habit of telling us the exact colour of every character he introduces'.[9] The novelist's answer would be that he is describing a society stratified along racial lines. However, division into black and white not only simplifies, but also polarises, issues. While all the whites oppose Josiah, practically no black man supports his opponents. Even the 'fiercely independent' Miss Martha Lee, a compound mixture of so many races, is forced to take a position on the colour spectrum on the island; a black sergeant silently compliments her: 'big job and all and pretty enough to claim to be Chinese; but no she doesn't claim to be coloured or Chinese coloured or any of those fancy ways of denying the blackness in her. She comes straight out with the blackness in her.'[10] Josiah, who is strikingly light brown, 'had projected so strongly the image of himself as a black man that everybody accepted him as a black man'.[11]

A novelist who is less concerned with individuals but uses people to represent or personify concepts cannot give a satisfactory treatment of society. Abrahams seems to be dealing less with people in society than with society as illustrated in certain abstracted characteristics. This is what makes it so easy for Josiah to accomplish his revolution. By making each character stand for a concept, the defeat of the character is made to look like the overthrow of that concept. By taming the Isaacs family Josiah subdues the foreign mercantile community; the forced retirement of Stanhope and the exile of Johnson means the defeat of an independent civil service and a free press respectively, just as surely as the detention of Justice Wright spells the doom of an independent judiciary. Although they are all very shrewd men Josiah's opponents are either too greedy (as with the Isaacs family), or too noble (Chief Justice Douglas Wright), or lacking in any power base (John Stanhope and Maxwell Johnson), to gang up against him. They do not receive any support from their professional colleagues. Furthermore, at no time does Josiah take on more than one opponent. This is not just political sagacity on his part, although we are told that he can 'outpolitic and out-manipulate' his adversaries at any time. The novelist must be pronounced guilty of aiding and abetting the President by isolating his opponents. Even within the cabinet, where we would normally expect alignments based on political convictions, Abrahams dwells only on personal characteristics. There are no political beliefs, no ideologies. Such characters belong to the world of caricature, not of serious public affairs. It is thus fortunate for the success of *This Island Now* that Abrahams makes Josiah's triumph over his Cabinet rivals come so early in the novel and it is so complete that after their first Cabinet business meeting we never hear of them again.

A general characteristic of this novel is that all the characters dwell in almost complete isolation. The only person who tries to reach out to another person is Andrew (Andy) Simpson, but his love affair with Sarah, the Chief Justice's daughter, is blighted by her father's refusal to go along with the socio-political revolution. Otherwise no other character has connections beyond his professional interests. Having buried his wife and child on the island (in circumstances which suggest that Abrahams merely copied Jones' family misfortunes from *A Wreath*), Johnson's life is his newspaper. Stanhope dines out occasionally, but his constant companion is his dog, given to him by the late President, whose wife receives only a passing mention in the story, but who otherwise has left no children or friends behind.

It is difficult to imagine a satisfactory public drama where characters are not seen in their relationships with each other. A critic who considers *This Island Now* inferior to Abrahams' other works gives as his reason: 'In the second part of the novel individual characters fade away, and personal relationships are banished from the narrative while the interest focuses on the dialectics of power.'[12] However, there is no doubt that Abrahams engineers this deliberately. Its epic and archetypal simplicities, which give *This Island Now* the character of a fable or a parable, strengthen it as a political novel. We are not witnessing private quarrels, motivated by personal vendetta. As Josiah hastens to assure Maxwell Johnson, the issues are extra-personal, indeed, global. The conflicts of the whole world are being rehearsed on a tiny island.

> ... You are primarily concerned with the salvation of your individual soul. I am not that free. Between me and your kind of freedom stands a terrible wall which I and those like me cannot climb until we have achieved the salvation of our racial soul. Till then

your concern about your individual soul is a rare and enviable luxury which I recognise longingly and then put behind me. Till then we cannot be individuals in the sense that you are and until we are all relations between white and coloured must be counterfeit by definition.[13]

This Island Now is truly a political novel. It attempts to analyse political motives, actions and their consequences. Josiah's predecessor, Moses Joshua, who combined in his own person such highly symbolic names, was the classic type of dictator. His personal rule was both long and complete enough to have earned him the paternalistic awesome title of the Old Man. 'He had straddled the island as unquestioned leader for nearly half a century.'[14] Yet, because—characteristically—he had not groomed a successor, his passing was also complete, a total break, like 'time coming to an abrupt stop, or the light of the sun being suddenly extinguished'.[15] One of Abrahams' achievements in this novel is to dramatise the gap between hope and reality, between effort and achievement. There could be no clean slate. The late President and, before him, the colonial regime that made his ascendancy possible, had committed the island to a political future from which it can be wrenched only with the greatest faith—and the greatest agony.

The incident when the opposition tried to make an issue of the Old Man's gift of a road to a favourite is an example of Abrahams' subtle understanding of the interplay of power politics. The President's opponents had attempted to rally the country against him by tabling a motion of no-confidence in Parliament, and outside it charging the President with acting like a dictator.

At an enormous function in the banqueting hall of the city's largest hotel, a mainly black tie affair, where chicken and wine were served, the spokesmen of the opposition had sent out a rallying call to the nation to rise up and man the barricades and hurl back and destroy the creeping dictatorship of the Joshua regime. But the mass of the people could not afford to go to the great hotel to hear the call to the barricades. Besides, they said to each other, the Old Man was not doing anything new. He had been doing this sort of thing for as long as they could remember. So why the fuss now? And when the no-confidence motion came up in parliament the Old Man had appeared at the door of the Chamber, wiggled the index finger of his right hand at the Members on the government benches, laughed out loud and poked out his tongue at the Opposition benches. The government Ministers had risen and solemnly marched out of the Chamber followed by their backbenchers. The Chairman of the Chamber had been forced to adjour the session for want of a quorum. And that was the end of the no-confidence motion, and it was also the end of the opposition. By making a joke of it the Old Man had destroyed the opposition utterly. So, when the one-party law was passed later, it merely legalised reality.[16]

The result of the opposition's action is exactly the opposite of what they had expected. But Abrahams insists that all are to blame: the dictatorial President, the apathetic people, the inept opposition, and the cowardly selfish parliamentarians—and all would suffer, not only during Joshua's regime, but far beyond. Through the inexorable movement of history, the Old Man had committed the island to a definite path: his rule had made certain that he would be followed by another dictator, not only because he had destroyed the opposition but also because after close to half a century of one-man rule, the situation favours the continuation of a dictatorship, the only form of government known to all the island. In addition, the Old Man's government by personal caprice prepared the way for the ascendancy of Josiah, the only one among the ministers who seemed to possess the semblance of a programme, the only independent spirit in this collection of ciphers.

As long as he had his own way, President Joshua had allowed the different groups on the island to go their different ways, a situation which in reality favoured the white and coloured classes who, because of their education, their colour, and their privileges inherited from the colonial period,

137

have been unconsciously exploiting the mass of the islanders. The liberal Jew, Joel Sterning, says: 'You, the brown-skinned élite, and the white mercantile and plantation crowd have literally brought Josiah about with your bloody ultra-conservatism.'[17] Indeed, Josiah's first victims are the white merchants ('the margin-gatherers', he contemptuously calls them), and the brown-skinned élite who dominate the civil service. His programme to effect 'a new pattern of power relations in which more value and importance and honour will be accorded to those people who contribute more to the productive wealth of the nation',[18] is calculated to bring him into conflict with the entrenched power-groups on the island. He successfully breaks the strangle-hold which the foreign mercantile companies have exercised on the island's economy by forcing them into a partnership with the government. Others whom he feels he doesn't need he just sweeps out of the way, like the Coloured Stanhope who is replaced with his deputy, Andy Simpson, a 'very tall, very suave, very handsome and very young diplomat in the making',[19] long a member of Josiah's innermost caucus. The liberal white Max Johnson is replaced as editor of *The Voice of The Island* by a veteran black journalist, the news editor of the state-controlled radio station, hitherto regarded as too radical. 'The new editor was a man committed to the ideas and principles Josiah was working to translate into practice: there was real understanding and respect between them. He assured the President of the paper's cooperation as long as he occupied the editor's chair.'[20]

Like the Presidency, says Josiah, every institution within the society 'must be an instrument of change serving the political will'.[21] To this end, even the armed forces are brought into line. Josiah's position, ably argued by Simpson his *alter ego*, is that there had never been any free institutions on the island but each had been used to serve certain special interests ; now, for a change, Josiah wants to use them to serve the people, in the interest of making life better for them. For the vast majority of the islanders—hungry, homeless, and illiterate—the concept of free institutions has no meaning whatsoever. Shouldn't they be made to trade that for the realities of life? Andy replies:

... It depends on which are the really key free institutions. When your belly is full and you live in a nice house and your children are in good schools and you have running water and electric light and you can call in your doctor whenever there is sickness you are likely to have a very different sense of values from the man who is hungry and homeless and whose children are not in school and who cannot get adequate medical attention. The values of free speech and free institutions are relative. There are people—not only here but all over what has become known as the third world—who will happily trade free speech and free institutions for three square meals a day, a roof over their heads and reasonable health services. Are you prepared to say they would be making such a bad trade?[22]

This is really a rhetorical question for Josiah who has decided that for the sake of his political revolution all other causes must give way. 'In our context,' he says, 'a show of strength is a very good thing and you can never overdo a good thing.'[23] So, when the privileged classes hardest hit by his programme brace for the fight Josiah deals with them in such a way as to score maximum political advantages. 'It is something big,' he exultantly tells a follower on the phone. 'The opportunity to make our show of strength.'[24] To Josiah the legal niceties of the case are least important; he is ready, even before the accused are tried, to promise to reprieve them since this gesture would serve political ends: symbolically it would be important to the black majority of the islanders to see 'the black President of a black country, to decide, as an act of mercy, to spare the life of a descendant of a slave-owner'.[25] Josiah is not interested in power for its own sake; even without his own testimony we know he is not a blood-thirsty tyrant; he is more interested in the ends to which political power can be put. To the chiefs of the security forces he spells out these ends.

Never forget for a moment ... that primarily this is a political trial with very clearly defined aims. First, it will assert our authority in the land unmistakably for all our enemies to see, those at home and those abroad, and there will be no more plots and conspiracies. Second, it will make plain to all investors, foreign and local, that this is a break with our colonial past and that capital, foreign and local, will no longer be permitted to manipulate power in this land. The great powers will get our message too, and it will be up to them to decide what they will do about it. Third, and most important of all, this trial must make it clear to the people in the hills and in the villages and in the fields and in the little shacks that this is their government exercising power on their behalf. They must see this trial as the assertion of their interests, the interests of the down-trodden and the dispossessed and the black, against the interests of the rich and the powerful and the fair. If the trial achieves these aims it will be justified; it will represent a twenty-year leap forward in the struggle to implant the *idea* of real independence. We will then be able to put most of our energies into the struggle to create economic independence. Fail in these aims and the trial becomes the pointless act of cruelty our critics are going to make it seem in any case. That is all I have to say, gentlemen. Much will depend on your handling of it. And in legal terms it must be above criticism.[26]

Josiah's confrontation with the judiciary is certainly the most arresting incident in the book; it also, appropriately, comes last, for of all the institutions in the land, the judiciary is the last stronghold of individual freedom. The confrontation assumes the dimensions of a conflict between two forces, two different ways of life, with the Justice representing the past—the tried, the known, and the certain—and the President representing the future, with all its uncertainty, more than a little tinged with elements of the reckless. 'The rule of law,' the Justice tells the President, 'must never depend on the strength or weakness of the position of the ruler. It must be constant, above person and position,'[27] meaning in effect that the Justice does not consider a political show of strength synonymous with good justice. He refuses, 'for any reason, to surrender the independence of the judiciary to political expedience'.[28] Thus, Josiah is forced to use the show of strength against the judiciary. Since he is a native son and thus cannot be exiled, the Justice is detained, thus establishing the validity of the dictum uttered by Max Johnson at his own departure: 'only native sons and daughters bear the full brunt'[29] of revolutions. After the Chief Justice, three other justices prove intractable, but once Wright is detained, one of them reneges, is assigned to the case and, the following week, is made the Acting President of the island's Supreme Court. On radio and television, Josiah explains in tears his reasons for detaining the island's most illustrious son: 'We are not against him ... It is only that we love the nation and its children more. We cannot allow even this great and honourable man to stand in the way of the nation.'[30]

With the defeat of the mercantile community, the civil service, the press, and the judiciary, there are no social institutions left standing in the way of Josiah's revolution—except the people it was designed to benefit. The apathy of the people had been demonstrated well enough in the past: when the opposition party wanted to make an issue of President Moses Joshua's gift of the road to Clara Sterning, for example. 'Traditionally they're on the side of the government, whichever it is; on the side of authority, of law and order, call it what you will.'[31] Under Joshua they had toiled contentedly for almost fifty years; then for three days after his death, nearly a third of them had filed in tears past his coffin. Simpson had said then in embittered anger: 'They are sick in the way all brain-washed people are sick. They don't know what they are doing. So much of their humanity, of their dignity, has been destroyed that they are afraid of standing on their own.'[32] But the land and the people had continued to stand behind the President as long as he had to take only political decisions. 'In those days his rule had shown all the hallmarks of a people's government and you can sense the pride and the confidence and the new-found self-assurance of the nation.'[33] Even the bad press received outside the country had been very useful in uniting the country, and 'honest fence-sitters', such as Martha Lee, have been constrained by the adverse publicity to move closer to the government.

But Josiah had run into trouble with the second phase, 'the assault on the economic problems' (Abrahams' new interest in economics reflects his position as editor of the *West Indian Economist*). In a mixture of idealism and naïvety, he had expected the people 'to give some of their labour to the nation, for the good of the nation, without being paid'.[34] But a show of strength had to be used, resulting in a week of rioting which left over two hundred dead. 'Perhaps they have been promised for too long that there were easy ways out of situations like this. There is no way out except through hard work.'[35] But there is also no way out except through Albert Josiah. Thus, for fear that the people may reject their saviour, referendums were stage-managed and elections suspended. The umbilical cord which linked the President with his people, acting as a conduit of nourishment, had been snapped.

In a long reverie towards the end of the story, Josiah, alone and unable to sleep, surveys his accomplishments, dwelling on the loss of his people's loyalty, a loss which gives a taste of ashes to his achievements:

> And the more he did, the more withdrawn his people became, the higher the invisible wall of cold-ness between them and him. As though he were the enemy.
> ... I was prepared for everything except this ...
> Sitting by the open window in his unlit bedroom Josiah took careful stock of the situation. He had conquered all his enemies, all those who stand in the way of the great revolution, and then his people had turned sour on him. How? Why? He had explained to them what the revolution meant, he had written it down for them, the party had conducted political classes throughout the country. But still the sourness was there. And he knew it would not be long before this sourness would express itself as opposition. And so, he knew, it was inevitable, only a matter of time, before he would have to be as harsh with the people as he had been with their enemies. For the job of creating a proud and independent island people, standing on their own feet, had only begun. The

great battle was still ahead. It would have been glorious fighting it with his people solidly behind him. It would be hard and it would hurt to have to use the party and the police and the military and the security to drive them.

... It will be hard. It will be done ...

And for a moment, there in the moonlight, feeling as lonely as he had ever felt, doubt came to Albert Josiah. And fear touched him. And the thought that this way might be wrong; that this was not the road to freedom for his people.

But if this was not the way then there was no way. The lion does not lie down peacefully with the lamb. The exploiters do not suffer a change of heart and cease to exploit. The great powers do not suddenly discover a morality that tells them it is wrong to manipulate small countries and use their lands as bases and battlefields and their people as living targets in the power game of showing muscle. If this way is wrong then there is no way out for the peoples of the so-called underdeveloped world. The people of that other world were lucky; they had had centuries in which to work out their institutions and had to grow rich and strong and stable: and of course they had the resources of the underdeveloped world, human and material, at their ready disposal. And in spite of their lip service today they are still bent on exploitation: subtler and more sophisticated it is true, but no less real for that.[36]

Is Abrahams on the side of Albert Josiah? A hard and rhetorical question, like other questions raised in the course of the story. Josiah's dialectical reading of history has by a deductive approach led to a conclusion which is diametrically opposed to Abrahams' stand in his earlier novels. For Josiah's conclusion is that there is no other way, the way of freedom, for the black people to regain their self-respect and sense of identity. The more important question is, if there is no other way, how have we got to this point of no return? This is the question that Andy Simpson asks as he crouches with a telescopic rifle to kill his erstwhile mentor: 'How did we get to the point where this has to be done? Whose failure? His? Ours?'[37] The answer to Andy's musing is the same as that to Josiah's flicks of doubt. The fault is not anybody's, but lies deep in history.

Abrahams seems to be saying that modernisation is incompatible with individual freedom. This puts him in agreement with Josiah's rationale for controlling personal freedom. Would Abrahams agree to the corollary that history has therefore destined the way of dictatorship for the underdeveloped countries? Certainly, he is saying that these countries have been caught in a vicious circle which it would be very difficult to break. The historical refrain that runs through the story, put in the mouth of Martha Lee, is: 'Things are never as simple and clearcut as the shakers and the shapers and revolution-makers would have us believe. There are no interest-free shortcuts. If you skip a stage in one way, you pay for it in another.'[38] Andy Simpson, to whom this warning is uttered, did not understand the full implications of the revolution on which he had embarked, and therefore fell by the wayside. 'Tell me,' Andy had asked Marthe Lee, 'how we can do a job, which I know you and I agree needs to be done, without soiling our hands?'[39] But only Josiah is fully aware of the amount of soiling that would accrue, the enormous price that has to be paid, and it is a tribute to his courage that he does not shy away from the problem or its solution, even when he loses the support of the masses which means so much to him. 'Not things he would have chosen to do; things forced on him if he is to carry through the great work of his life, the liberating of the land and its people.'[40]

Josiah has come adequately prepared for his mission. In times like this the saviour must be like Josiah, 'full of faith and no love'. His faith in the people of the island is the type that has moved mountains. 'All that mankind has achieved thus far on earth has been based on this kind of faith. Without it very little could have been done.'[41] Josiah had tried to make his faith propel the island forward along the path of progress; he loses faith in the people—but never in himself, nor in his mission—when he discovers that they are not a mass but an aggregate of fallible and petty human beings. Faced with the same hopeless dilemma between personal freedom and the exorbitant price that must be paid to win final racial recognition, the independent-minded Martha Lee grudgingly casts her vote for the suppression of personal freedom; for Martha, like her creator, would not agree that nothing should be done to change conditions. The price may be heavy but it has to be paid.

And *This Island Now* leaves us in no doubt about the extremely heavy cost and the wide array of people paying it. 'In our context,' Andy had confidently predicted to Martha at the beginning, 'to act in the interest of the people is to offend someone, some special interest. No matter what we do, someone will cry tyranny.'[42] By the end of the story, but put at the beginning of the novel—a successful attempt to portray the irony of fortune that is such a strong theme in the novel—the people are mumbling tyranny against a revolution designed for their own good. Adds Abrahams: 'Once this earth had communicated a high sense of freedom to its children, especially in the years immediately after the withdrawal of the occupying power. Now fear was a long shadow over the land and its children.'[43] A novelist more knowledgeable in the ways of revolutions has written: 'Hopes grotesquely betrayed, ideals caricatured—that is the definition of revolutionary success.'[44]

Could Abrahams, by using more complex characters instead of fable figures, have more convincingly argued his case that modernisation must be inevitably accompanied by dictatorship? It is probable that a political point of view can be argued only in the simplicity of the black-and-white characters that he has used. Could he have reached different conclusions if he had created a sense of society complete with the continuities of social living? *This Island Now* fails as a first-class political novel because it does not maintain a balance of interrelation between character, psychology, political ideas and political actions, because it does not allow a variety of personal political motives. On the other hand, by including such details, the novel would have lost the intensity of its conflicts and the poignancy of its dilemma. Indeed, both its strengths and weaknesses are inseparably interwoven.

NOTES

¹ *This Island now* (Faber and Faber, London, 1966). All page references are to this edition.

² *Ibid.*, p. 150.   ⁶ *Ibid.*, p. 97.
³ *Ibid.*, p. 193.   ⁷ *Ibid.*, p. 185.
⁴ *Ibid.*, p. 219.   ⁸ *Ibid.*, p. 237.
⁵ *Ibid.*, p. 154.

⁹ Prima Lewis, '*Politics and the Novel*', in *Zuka*, 2 (May, 1968), p. 44.
¹⁰ *Ibid.*, p. 46.
¹¹ *Ibid.*, p. 159.
¹² Hena Maes-Jelinek, *Race Relations and Identity in Peter Abrahams' 'Pluralia'*, in *English Studies* (February, 1969), p. 111.

¹³ *Ibid.*, p. 211.   ²⁹ *Ibid.*, p. 242.
¹⁴ *Ibid.*, p. 15.   ³⁰ *Ibid.*, p. 244.
¹⁵ *Ibid.*, p. 15.   ³¹ *Ibid.*, p. 31.
¹⁶ *Ibid.*, p. 24.   ³² *Ibid.*, p. 51.
¹⁷ *Ibid.*, p. 118.   ³³ *Ibid.*, p. 249.
¹⁸ *Ibid.*, p. 96.   ³⁴ *Ibid.*, p. 249.
¹⁹ *Ibid.*, p. 50.   ³⁵ *Ibid.*, p. 250.
²⁰ *Ibid.*, p. 244.   ³⁶ *Ibid.*, pp. 251–2
²¹ *Ibid.*, p. 210.   ³⁷ *Ibid.*, p. 91.
²² *Ibid.*, pp. 144–5.   ³⁸ *Ibid.*, p. 145.
²³ *Ibid.*, p. 221.   ³⁹ *Ibid.*, p. 144.
²⁴ *Ibid.*, p. 201.   ⁴⁰ *Ibid.*, pp. 252–3.
²⁵ *Ibid.*, p. 221.   ⁴¹ *Ibid.*, p. 145.
²⁶ *Ibid.*, pp. 217–18.   ⁴² *Ibid.*, p. 144.
²⁷ *Ibid.*, p. 237.   ⁴³ *Ibid.*, p. 11.
²⁸ *Ibid.*, p. 234.

⁴⁴ Joseph Conrad, *Under Western Eyes* (Methuen, London, 1924), p. 135.

Conclusion

I am a child of the plural societies. When the
strains and pressures had grown too much for me, I
had escaped from the physical presence of the problem. But the problem itself is inescapable. It will be
with me either till it is resolved or till the end of my
days. It is the raw material of my work. The most
challenging, the most exciting raw material in the
world—and also, in one sense, the most inhibiting.[1]

Abrahams, in his novels, has fashioned his own response,
both stylistic and moral, to the socio-political problems of
South Africa. As with all writers, what he believes has influenced what he wrote, both in its subject and its tone and
stance. Abrahams shares the liberal belief that it is only in the
hearts of individuals that freedom from racism must come
about. He has remained consistent in his belief that in the final
analysis the problem can only be satisfactorily settled on the
personal level. And the solution he has proposed has more
validity on the personal rather than the societal level: people
must understand and accept each other as individuals.

Even after his visit to South Africa in 1952 jolted him into
taking a more political stance, Abrahams' political philosophy
was greatly tempered by his liberal beliefs. In 1956, immediately after he published *A Wreath*, he commended the traditional African societies for lacking in colour consciousness:

Being black is a small matter in tribal Africa
because the attitude to colour is healthy and normal.
Colour does not matter. Colour is an act of God that
neither confers privileges nor imposes handicaps on
a man. A man's skin is like the day: the day is either
clear or dark. There is nothing more to it until external agencies come in and invest it with special meaning and importance. What does matter to the tribal
African, what is important, is the complex pattern of

his position within his own group and his relations with the other members of the group. He is no Pan-African dreaming of a greater African glory when the white man is driven into the sea. The acute race consciousness of the American Negro, or of the black South African at the receiving end of apartheid, is alien to him. The important things in his life are anything but race and colour—until they are forced on him.[2]

However, Westernisation, which Abrahams recommended as the panacea for the evils of tribalism has thrust racial and colour consciousness within the psychological horizon of the black man. Increased racial contact and the spread of education, far from improving the situation throughout the world, have provided additional occasions for racial friction and intensified awareness of racial difference, leading to rejection by non-whites of the assumption that the white man's ways are the yardstick for civilisation. Yet, there is no way of diminishing the areas of racial contact in the world today. Abrahams has bowed to the reality that all over the world the non-white will continue to view the white man with hostility until he can prove himself to be his equal and is accepted as such. This is why he concludes in *This Island Now* that the black man must first assert his racial identity before he can be free to forget it.

With this awareness, Abrahams believes that the solution to the racial problem will be difficult and long drawn-out. He opts for evolution not revolution, to build by love, not to destroy by anger. In a 1965 essay significantly titled *We Can Learn to be Colour-Blind*, Abrahams took stock of the mutual acrimony between white and black occasioned by the crisis in the Congo (Zaire), and pronounced that the colour problem derived from the fact that a majority of mankind, both Afro-Asians and Westerners, do not accord each other 'a qualitatively equal humanity'. Yet, he added, it would be most surprising if it were otherwise, considering the hostility between the darker and lighter races over the last three hundred years. All the same, Abrahams remains optimistic about the future:

All this is on the assumption that our generation does not make such a mess of things that when the new generation takes over they find a wall of colour so high that all real communication is impossible.

I think the only way to make sure that we do not make such a mess is to keep on talking and thinking about the problems we face and to go on seeking ways and means of making the kinds of human contacts across oceans and continents that will make each man recognise the rare and distinctive humanity of every other man. I do not think there is any pat or slick or easy answer. This has to do with that most important of all man's journeys through the ages, the long march to self-knowledge, which has been such an important driving force in all he has done so far in his life here on earth.

Like all really fundamental challenges there are no simple political or economic or ideological solutions to this one. It embraces all these and more because it has to do with the way men look at each other. I think the realisation of this is an important beginning.[3]

Abrahams, preoccupied with the necessity to establish an appropriate attitude towards the political situation not only in South Africa but all over the world, preaches that love is the only weapon that can overcome the hatred represented by the colour bar. Even non-whites who are driven towards hatred admit the superiority of love. Says the 'authorial' character, Mako, in *The Path of Thunder*: 'I want to like other people too, but how can I like those who are hard on my people? I must fight them. And when we are free, then I will learn to love them.'[4] And Josiah in *This Island Now* thinks that the black man cannot be primarily concerned with the salvation of his individual soul until he and his people have achieved the salvation of their racial soul. 'Till then we cannot be individuals in the sense that the whites are and until we are all relations between white and coloured must be counterfeit by definition.'[5] Abrahams' characters talk in this fashion because they have faith in the future; as a part of the oppressed majority, they have the force of morality at their back. Because they are already sure of victory, even if it doesn't come in their own lifetime, Abrahams' characters do not voice the despair common in most novels by the oppressed. For this reason Abrahams' novels will probably survive the present mood of confrontation.

NOTES

[1] *Return to Goli*, p. 29
[2] *An African Treasury*, ed. Langston Hughes (Gollancz, London, 1961), p. 44.
[3] *New York Times Magazine*, April 11, 1965, p. 107.
[4] *The Path of Thunder*, p. 95.
[5] *This Island Now*, p. 211.

A Selected Bibliography

Primary Sources

Books

American dates of publication are given only when they influence the order of appearance of Abrahams' books.

Dark Testament (short stories)
George Allen and Unwin Ltd, London, 1942.

Song of the City (novel)
Dorothy Crisp and Co., London, 1945.

Mine Boy (novel)
Dorothy Crisp and Co., London, 1946.
Faber and Faber, London, 1954.
Heinemann Educational Books, London, 1963.

The Path of Thunder (novel)
Harper, New York, 1948.
Faber and Faber, London, 1952.

Wild Conquest (novel)
Harper, New York, 1950.
Faber and Faber, London, 1951.

Return to Goli (documentary)
Faber and Faber, London, 1953.

Tell Freedom (autobiography)
Faber and Faber, London, 1954
Collier-Macmillan, New York, 1970.

A Wreath for Udomo (novel)
Faber and Faber, London, 1956.

Jamaica: *An Island Mosaic* (documentary)
Her Majesty's Stationery Office (Corona Library Series), London, 1957.

A Night of Their Own (novel)
Faber and Faber, London, 1965.

This Island Now (novel)
Faber and Faber, London, 1966.

Essays

Colonialism on Trial: *The Kenyatta Case*, in *The Nation*, 177 (July 11, 1953), pp. 31–2.

The Conflict of Cultures in Africa, in *International Affairs*, XXX:3 (July, 1954), pp. 304–12.

The Blacks, in *Holiday*, 25 (April, 1959), pp. 2–4, 74–5, 118–26. Reprinted in abbreviated form in *An African Treasury*, ed. Langston Hughes, Gollancz, London, 1961, pp. 42–55.

Manifesto from Johannesburg, in *Saturday Review*, 42 (August 1, 1959), pp. 22–3.

The Meaning of Harlem, in *Holiday*, 27 (June 1960), pp. 74–81, 136–42.

The Puerto Ricans, in *Holiday*, 29 (February, 1961), pp. 33–47, 132–41.

New Faces from Africa, in *Holiday*, 31 (April, 1962), pp. 92–102.

The Real Jamaica, in *Holiday*, 33 (March, 1963), pp. 96–9, 102–4, 178–89.

We Can Learn To Be Colour-Blind, in *New York Times Magazine* (April 11, 1965), pp. 38, 102–7.

Reviews

BO	Black Orpheus.
CSM	Christian Science Monitor.
CSTMB	Chicago Sunday Times Magazine of Books.
LJ	Library Journal.
MG	The Manchester Guardian.
NR	New Republic.
NSN	New Statesman and Nation.
NY	New Yorker.
NYTBR	New York Times Book Review.
NYHTRB	New York Herald Tribune Book Review.
NYHTWR	New York Herald Tribune Weekly Review.
SR	Saturday Review.
SRL	Saturday Review of Literature.

ST	The Sunday Times.
TLS	The Times Literary Supplement.
YL	Yale Review.

Dark Testament

TLS	January 16, 1943, p. 34.

Mine Boy

TLS	October 5, 1940, p. 477.
TLS	September 24, 1954, p. 615.
NYTBR	June 12, 1955, p. 5.
NYHTBR	June 12, 1955, p. 2.
NY	31 (June 18, 1955), pp. 93–4.
NR	132 (June 27, 1955), p. 20.
CSM	June 30, 1955, p. 9.
SR	38 (July 2, 1955), pp. 18–19.
CSTMB	July 31, 1955, p. 3.
Yl	n.s. 45 (Autumn, 1955), pp. 254–5.

The Path of Thunder

NY	23 (February 7, 1948), p. 85.
NYHTWR	February 8, 1948, p. 13.
NYTBR	February 8, 1948, p. 5.
SRL	31 (February 14, 1948), pp. 25–6.
CSM	March 27, 1948, p. 13.
TLS	March 21, 1952, p. 201.

Wild Conquest

NYTBR	April 30, 1950, p. 4.
NYHTBR	May 14, 1950, p. 6.
NY	26 (May 27, 1950), p. 97.
SRL	33 (June 17, 1950), p. 21.
NR	122 (June 26, 1950), p. 21.
ST	May 20, 1951, p. 3.
TLS	June 1, 1951, p. 337.

Return to Goli

TLS	June 12, 1953, p. 378.
America	91 (September 25, 1954), p. 622.

Tell Freedom

NSN	47 (June 19, 1954), p. 808.
LJ	79 (August, 1954), p. 1394.
NYTBR	August 8, 1954, p. 1.
NYHTBR	August 8, 1954, pp. 1, 12.
Newsweek	44 (August 9, 1954), p. 47–8.

SR	37 (August 14, 1954), pp. 10–11.
Nation	179 (August 21, 1954), p. 154.
MG	August 27, 1954, p. 4.
Atlantic	194 (September 1954), p. 81.
Commonwealth	60 (September 10, 1954), pp. 563–4.
NY	30 (September 11, 1954), p. 141.

A Wreath for Udomo

LJ	81 (May 1, 1956), p. 1183.
The Times	May 3, 1956, p. 13.
The Spectator	196 (May 11, 1956), p. 665.
NSN	51 (May 12, 1956), pp. 543–4.
TLS	May 18, 1956, p. 295.
NYTBR	May 20, 1956, pp. 5, 26.
SR	39 (May 26, 1956), p.15.
CSTMB	May 27, 1956, p. 7.
NYHTBR	June 3, 1956, p. 2.
CSM	June 28, 1956, p. 9.
Ny	32 (June 30, 1956), pp. 78, 81.
Commonwealth	64 (July 13, 1956), pp. 376–7.
BO	4 (October, 1958), pp. 56–8.

Jamaica: An Island Mosaic

TLS	January 10, 1958, p. 21.

A Night of Their Own

The Times	March 25, 1965, p. 15.
TLS	March 25, 1965, p. 229.
NS	69 (March 26, 1965), p. 501.
The Observer	March 28, 1965, p. 26.
NYTBR	April 11, 1965, p. 42.
Newsweek	65 (April 12, 1965), pp. 61–2.
Punch	248 (May 5, 1965), p. 676.
Bestsellers	25 (May 15, 1965), p. 88.
NY	41 (September 25, 1965), pp. 221–2.
BO	22 (August, 1967), pp. 59–60.

This Island Now

The Times	September 29, 1966, p. 16.
TLS	October 20, 1966, p. 964.
LJ	92 (July, 1967), p. 2600.
Bestsellers	27 (September 15, 1967), p. 236.
NYTBR	72 (September 24, 1967), p. 47.
America	11 (October 7, 1967), pp. 392–3.

Secondary Sources

Susan Anderson, *Something in me Died: Autobiographies of South African Writers in Exile*, in *Books Abroad*, XLIV:3 (Summer 1970), pp. 398–404.

Wilfred Cartey, *Whispers from a Continent; The Literature of Contemporary Black Africa*, Random House, New York, 1969.

A. Guérard, *Le Roman Néo-Africain—Peter Abrahams*, in *La Revue Nouvelle*, XXVIII (1963), pp. 374–81.
Peter Abrahams et la Littérature Sud-Africaine, in *La Revue Nouvelle*, XLV (1967), pp. 651–4.

Nadine Gordimer, *The Novel and the Nation in South Africa* in *The Times Literary Supplement*, August 11, 1961, pp. 520–30.

Christopher Heywood, *The Novels of Peter Abrahams*, in *Perspectives on African Literature*, ed. Heywood, Heinemann, London, 1971, pp. 157–72.

Vladimir Klima, *South African Prose Writing in English*, Publishing House of the Czechoslovak Academy of Sciences, Prague, 1971.

Charles Larson, *The Emergence of African Fiction*, Indiana University Press, Bloomington, Indiana, 1971.

C.T. Maduka, *Humanism and the South African Writer: Peter Abrahams' 'A Wreath for Udomo'*, in *Umoja*, n.s.I: 1 (1977), pp. 17–31.

Primila Lewis, *Politics and the Novel: An Appreciation of 'A Wreath for Udomo' and This Island Now'*, in *Zuka*, 2 (May, 1968), pp. 41–7.

G. M. Miller and Howard Sergeant, *A Critical Survey of South African Poetry in English*, Balkema, Capetown, 1957.

H. Maes-Jelinek, *Race Relations and Identity in Peter Abrahams' 'Pluralia'*, in *English Studies*, February, 1969, pp. 106–12.

Ezekiel Mphahlele, *The African Image*, Faber and Faber, London, 1962.
Variations on a Theme: Race and Colour, in *Présence Africaine*, 83, (1972), pp. 92–204.
Voices in the Whirlwind and Other Essays, Macmillan, London, 1973.

James Ngugi, *The Writer and His Past*, in *Homecoming*, ed. Ngugi wa Thiong'o, Heinemann, London, 1972, pp. 39–46.

Lewis Nkosi, *Fiction by Black South Africans*, in *Black Orpheus* 19, (1966), pp. 48–54.

Kolawole Ogungbesan, *The Political Novels of Peter Abrahams*, in *Présence Africaine*, 83 (1972), pp. 33–50.
The Path of Thunder: The Hope Next Time, in *Re: Arts and Letters*, VI:2 (Fall, 1972), pp. 15–27.
The Politics of 'This Island Now', in *Journal of Commonwealth Literature*, VIII:1 (June, 1973), pp. 33–41.
Peter Abrahams' 'Wild Conquest': In the Beginning was Conflict, in *Studies in Black Literature*, IV:2 (Summer, 1973), pp. 11–20.

John Povey, *The Political Theme in South and West African Novels*, in *African Quarterly* IX:1 (April–June 1969), pp. 33–9.
Non-European Writing in South Africa, in *Review of National Literatures*, II:2 (Fall, 1971), pp. 66–80.

Martin Tucker, *Africa in Modern Literature*, New York, 1967.

Michael Wade, *The Novels of Peter Abrahams*, in *Critique*, XI:3 (December, 1968), pp. 54–60.
Peter Abrahams, Evans, London, 1972.